W9-APN-292

Statistical Methods for the Information Professional

Statistical Methods for the Information Professional

A Practical, Painless Approach
to Understanding, Using, and
Interpreting Statistics

Liwen Vaughan

ASIST Monograph Series

Published for the
American Society for Information Science and Technology by

Information Today, Inc.
Medford, New Jersey

Fourth printing, March 2008

Statistical Methods for the Information Professional: A Practical, Painless Approach to Understanding, Using, and Interpreting Statistics

Copyright © 2001 by American Society for Information Science and Technology

All rights reserved. No part of this book may be reproduced in any form or by any electronic or mechanical means, including information storage and retrieval systems, without permission in writing from the publisher, except by a reviewer, who may quote brief passages in a review. Published by Information Today, Inc., 143 Old Marlton Pike, Medford, New Jersey 08055.

Library of Congress Cataloging-in-Publication Data

Vaughan, Liwen, 1956-
    Statistical methods for the information professional : a practical, painless approach to understanding, using, and interpreting statistics / Liwen Vaughan.
        p. cm. -- (ASIST monograph series)
    Includes bibliographical references and index.
    ISBN 1-57387-110-9
        1. Commercial statistics. I. Title. II. Series.
HF1017 . V38 2001
519.5--dc21

          2001016655

Publisher: Thomas H. Hogan, Sr.
Editor-in-Chief: John B. Bryans
Managing Editor: Janet M. Spavlik
Production Manager: M. Heide Dengler
Copy Editor: Pat Hadley-Miller
Designer: Anne S. Alexander
Indexer: Sharon Hughes

Printed in Canada

Table of Contents

List of Figures

List of Tables

Preface

Not Just Another Stats Book

It is remarkable that statistics is both one of most useful and powerful tools in data analysis and also one of the most feared and hated subjects of study. The root of this fear is that statistics books are usually filled with equations, mathematical jargon, and pages of derivations and calculations. What sets this book apart from so many others is its focus on understanding the basic logic of statistics rather than the mathematical intricacies. The emphasis is on the meaning of statistics, when to apply them, how to apply them, and how to interpret results. It reflects the highly successful approach that I have refined in my ten years of teaching statistics. There are three elements to this approach:

First of all, I use logical reasoning rather than mathematical deduction to explain statistical concepts and tests. While statistics is a branch of mathematics, the underlying logic of many statistical tests is very straightforward and requires no background in advanced mathematics to understand. The pages of equations and mathematical explanations commonly found in statistics books often obscure the simplicity of this underlying logic. Therefore, you will not see very many equations in this book. The few you do see will be carefully explained and can be ignored without harming your understanding of the basic principles being discussed.

Secondly, I use an example from information science research to demonstrate the complete process of each statistical test covered. I begin with how to formulate hypotheses, then cover the use of computer software to analyze the data, interpretation of the output, and reaching conclusions. Readers will see the complete picture of how statistical methods are applied rather than getting drowned in technical details. This emphasis on real applications of the statistical methods will enable the reader to see how statistics are a powerful and relevant tool rather than an arcane branch of mathematics irrelevant to them.

Finally, I emphasize the use of computer software to do calculations and other mathematical drudge work. Many statistics books spend a great deal of time on deriving formulae and carrying out calculations. The truth is that almost no one does these calculations manually today. There are a variety of computer software packages that can be used to take over the hard mathematical work so that we can focus on understanding the meaning of the results. In recognition of this, I have dedicated a chapter to issues that are specific to the use of computer software for doing statistical analysis.

I have used this approach to teach statistics to students in various disciplines at levels from undergraduate to doctoral. Most students in my classes had very little mathematical background and many entered the course with feelings of fear and nervousness. However, they were pleasantly surprised at how painless statistics can be and how exciting it is to understand a subject that was once mysterious and foreign to them. Indeed, it is a myth that statistics is complex and beyond people who are not mathematically oriented. I am confident that you will agree with me once you read this book.

Who Should Read this Book

Information professionals, both academics and practitioners, will find this book very useful in understanding the statistical concepts and techniques that are increasingly used in information science and appear extensively in the literature. As an information professional, you are at least a consumer of the statistical results produced by others even if you are not a producer of statistics yourself. The purpose of this book is to provide you with a resource to help in both understanding and utilizing statistical methods. Even if you are not an information professional, you can still benefit from reading the book. After all, the basic theories and principles of statistics are the same for any field.

How to Use this Book

This book covers basic statistical methods commonly used in information science research. These methods include descriptive statistics, the t test, chi-square test, analysis of variance, correlation, regression, and the basic non-parametric statistical tests. The book will also introduce some intermediate and advanced statistical methods such as multiple regression and LISREL.

If you are already familiar with statistical analysis in general and are using this book to refresh your memory on a particular subject, then you can just go directly to the section of the book that interests you. In particular, the summary chart given in Chapter 12 can be used to decide which test you need to review for a given situation so that you can then go to the appropriate chapter.

If you are learning statistics for the first time or if you learned it in the past but need to refresh your knowledge of the major concepts, then I recommend that you read the first six chapters in sequence before getting into other chapters. Chapter 1 discusses how to recognize different types of data, the very first issue you will encounter when you start data analysis. Chapter 2 deals with general issues of using computer software to do statistical analysis, including how to organize data into computer files and how to deal with missing data. Chapters 3 and 4 discuss graphs and descriptive statistics respectively. Chapter 5 introduces the basic concepts of inferential statistics. Because this chapter lays the foundation for all the statistical tests discussed in later chapters, it should be read before moving into later chapters. Chapter 6 covers various sampling methods.

While the nature of the subjects in the first six chapters requires a sequential reading, Chapters 7 through 11 do not have to be read in sequence because each chapter introduces a different statistical test. Therefore, you can move directly to a chapter that is of particular interest to you. Chapter 12 summarizes the inferential statistical tests covered in Chapters 7 through 11. The summary chart there is designed to be a "roadmap" guiding you to the right statistical test to use for your particular situation. Chapter 13 is an introduction to some intermediate to advanced statistical methods. It is recommended that you read this chapter last, since much of it builds on concepts introduced in earlier chapters.

Acknowledgments

I am very grateful to my husband David Vaughan for all his support, both spiritual and technical, on this book project. He carefully edited the entire book; painstakingly converted all the figures and tables to the required formats for publication; and, more importantly, acted as a sounding board for my ideas and thoughts. This book would have been impossible without his help. My son Ulysses was still in the womb when I began this project and was a toddler by the end, so that he literally grew up while I wrote. He is a source of constant inspiration. The book project often pulled me away from my family duties and I am deeply in debt to David and Ulysses. This book is dedicated to them.

CHAPTER 1

Getting Started— Recognizing the Types of Data

Just as we must classify and organize information before it can be retrieved and used, we must classify data into the correct type before we can do any statistical analysis on them. The data type will determine how data must be coded for analysis and what kinds of analysis can be performed. Any data can be classified into one of four types: nominal, ordinal, interval, and ratio. These four data types are the results of measuring variables in the four corresponding measurement scales: nominal scale, ordinal scale, interval scale, and ratio scale. To explain how to recognize the four types of data, let us look at Figure 1-1, which shows a hypothetical questionnaire for an Internet user survey.

1.	Gender	Female _____	Male _____
2.	Postal code of your home address _____		
3.	How would you rate the quality of our service?		
	Poor ____ Fair _____ Average _____ Good _____ Excellent _____		
4.	How many points have you cumulated from our bonus point program? _____		
5.	How many e-mail messages did you send yesterday? _____		
6.	How old are you as of your last birthday? _____ years old		
7.	What is your yearly income?		
	Under $20,000 _____		
	$20,000 to $29,999 _____		
	$30,000 to $39,999 _____		
	$40,000 to $49,999 _____		
	$50,000 to $59,999 _____		
	$60,000 and over _____		

Figure 1-1   Sample Questions from a Survey Conducted by an Internet Provider

1.1 Nominal Data

The answers to question #1 will be either "female" or "male." Before we can input these responses into statistical software for analysis, we must code them by assigning a number to each possible answer. We can code female as 1 and male as 2 or vice versa. This coding is purely arbitrary and symbolic, therefore the calculations that we can do on these data are limited. We cannot calculate the average of these 1s and 2s because the result will be meaningless (the average person is somebody between a male and a female?). We can only count the frequency of 1s and 2s to find out how many respondents are males and how many are females. This type of data is called nominal data. **Nominal data are obtained when numbers are used to arbitrarily label categories. The only calculation that can be applied to nominal data is to note the frequency of occurrence of each category**.

The second question, postal code, is often asked to find out in which neighborhood the survey respondent resides. The postal codes obtained can be mapped into individual neighborhoods, which are then labeled with numbers, e.g., northeast labeled with 1, northwest labeled with 2, etc. As with the gender data discussed above, the numbers are being assigned arbitrarily and cannot be used in meaningful calculations other than simple counting. Therefore, the postal codes and the neighborhoods derived from them are also nominal data.

1.2 Ordinal Data

The third question asks survey respondents to rate the quality of the service in a five-point scale, i.e., in five categories. We can code the answers to the question in the following ways: 1 for poor, 2 for fair, 3 for average, 4 for good, and 5 for excellent; or we can reverse the order and code 1 for excellent and 5 for poor. In the former coding method, the higher the number the better the quality; in the latter coding method, the lower the number the better. However, we cannot code 1 for poor, 2 for excellent, 3 for fair, etc. The coding is not completely arbitrary and must follow an order (from high to low or from low to high) to indicate the rank of quality inherent in the words used.

The data collected in this type of question are called ordinal data; i.e., the "quality of service" variable is measured in ordinal scale. Once a coding method is chosen, say 1 for poor to 5 for excellent, we know that 4 is of a better quality than 3, which in turn is better than 2. However, we cannot say that the quality difference between 1 and 2 is equal to that between 3 and 4. The numbers are attached simply to show the order—not to show how much better each is compared with others (Rowntree, 1981, 31). **Ordinal data contain information as to better or worse, or greater or less, but they do not tell us details as to how much better or how much greater**.

1.3 Interval Data

Question 4 introduces the third type of data, known as interval data. To see what constitutes interval data and why question 4 fits into this category, let us first look at the Celsius and Fahrenheit scales that are used to measure temperature. These temperature scales are used in many statistics books as classic examples of interval scales. When we measure temperature, we not only know that an object of 25°C is warmer than an object of 20°C but also know that it is exactly 5°C warmer. The temperature difference between these two objects is the same as the difference between 20°C and 15°C. However, we cannot say that an object of 20°C is twice as warm as an object of 10°C because temperature measured in Celsius does not have an absolute zero point. That is, the zero point is arbitrarily chosen and an object of 0°C is not without heat or molecular motion. The arbitrary nature of the zero point in Celsius is clearer if we consider Fahrenheit in which 32°F corresponds to 0°C. Saying that the two objects are 20°C and 10°C is equivalent to saying that they are 68°F and 50°F. Apparently, when we say that 20°C is twice as warm as 10°C, we cannot say the same for their corresponding Fahrenheit values: 68°F and 50°F (68 /50 ≠ 2). The reason is clear: both Celsius and Fahrenheit temperatures have arbitrary zero points. **Interval data provide not only greater-than-or-less-than information, but also details on how much greater than or less than. However, interval data have no absolute zero point, so that we CANNOT use comparisons such as "twice as many" or "half as much" with interval data.**

Question 4 of our example survey refers to the bonus point program set up to encourage the use of the service. The Internet service provider gives every user 2,000 points as soon as they sign up for the service and then gives 100 points for each dollar the user pays for the service. Users can claim various prizes based on the total number of bonus points accumulated. It is easy to see that the point system gives detailed information on how many more or less points any user has than any other user. A user with 3,000 points has 500 more points than a user with 2,500 points and this is the same as the difference between users with 5,000 and 4,500 points. What is more difficult is in seeing how the point system lacks an absolute zero. The key is that we are looking at points accumulated, not just points earned from dollars spent, so that the 2,000 base points are included in the total. Since every user has these 2,000 points, there is no absolute zero point because users' point totals really did not begin from zero. For example, a user who had accumulated 10,000 points has not earned twice as many points as a user with 5,000 points, because if you subtract the 2,000-point bonus that both of them received on signing, you then have 8,000 points versus 3,000 points, more than twice as many.

To give an example of interval data from the field of library and information science, we can look at library summer reading programs. Many public libraries organize summer reading programs for children. Children earn points for every book they read and can receive various prizes at the end of the program based on the number of points they have accumulated. In order to encourage kids to participate in the program and start reading, the library gives x number of points to every child who signs up for the program. For the same reasons given for the Internet provider's bonus program, the points accumulated in the program are interval data.

1.4 Ratio Data

Question 5 "How many e-mail messages did you send yesterday?" and Question 6 "How old are you as of your last birthday?" are examples of ratio data collection. They measure whether a given response is greater than or less than other responses and give details about how much greater or less. In addition, they have an absolute zero point. In Question 5, a user may have sent zero messages yesterday. We not only know that somebody who sent ten messages sent more messages than a person who sent five, but we also know that he/she sent twice as many messages. Similarly, we not only know that somebody who is 60 years old is older than a 20 year-old person, but also know that he/she is three times older. **Ratio data provide not only greater-than-or-less-than information, but also details on how much greater than or less than. In addition, there is an absolute and** non-arbitrary zero point so that we CAN use comparisons such as "twice as many."

Let us look at Question 4 again for a moment to clarify the difference between interval and ratio data. We had decided that the number of points accumulated by the users was interval data because of the granting of a 2,000-point signing bonus. However, if the provider does not grant bonus points for signing, then all users start at zero points and the points accumulated are ratio data. A user with 10,000 points really has earned twice as many points as a user with 5,000 points.

1.5 Data Conversion

What type of data does Question 7, "What is your yearly income?" collect? You may think that there is an absolute zero point for income; i.e., no income at all. A person whose income is $40,000 has twice as much income as somebody whose income is $20,000. Therefore, incomes are ratio data. However, when we look closely at what kind of answers we will get from Question 7, it is clear that the incomes collected here are not ratio data. The survey asks respondents to place themselves into one of the six categories of income. We can code these six categories from 1 to 6 with 1 for the lowest income category and 6 for the highest income category. If John is in the fourth category and Jane fits into the second category, we know that John's income is higher than Jane's but we do not know exactly how much higher because both categories include a range of incomes. Although John's answer will be coded as 4 and Jane's as 2, we cannot say that John's income is twice as high as Jane's. Therefore, Question 7 collects ordinal data.

Here we see a very important point on data classification. It is not only the variable itself that determines the type of data but also how we collect the data, e.g., how we solicit the responses in a survey. If the survey asks respondents to provide their incomes in dollar figures, then the income data collected will be ratio data. If the survey asks respondents' income range, as in Question 7 above, then the income data collected will be ordinal data. The same is true for the age variable often encountered in surveys. If we ask a survey respondent's exact age, as in the case of Question 6 above, then ages are ratio data. If we ask respondents to indicate the age group (e.g., 20 to 29, 30 to 39, etc.) to which they belong, then ages become ordinal data.

What type of data (ratio or ordinal) should be collected in this kind of situation? The principle is that if ratio data are available, then collect ratio data. There are two reasons for this choice. First, if we collect ratio data and later decide that we want ordinal data, we can always convert the former into the latter. However, if we collect ordinal data we cannot convert them into ratio data later. For example, if we know people's exact income figures, we can always fit these figures into income categories. However, we cannot do the reverse. The four types of data represent four levels of measurement with nominal being the lowest level, ordinal the second, interval the third, and ratio the highest. As a general rule, higher level data can be converted to a lower level but lower level data cannot be converted to a higher level.

There is another reason that interval or ratio data are preferred over nominal or ordinal data. Different types of statistical tests can be applied to different types of data. Parametric tests, which are generally more powerful tests, are usually used for interval or ratio data while nonparametric tests, which are less powerful, are usually used for nominal or ordinal data (don't worry about the new terms here, they will be discussed in later chapters). The point can be made even without resorting to discussion of parametric vs. nonparametric tests. Higher level data contain more information than the lower level data. When incomes are presented in exact dollar figures (ratio data), we not only know who has a higher income but also know exactly how much higher and how many times higher. When incomes are presented in income categories (ordinal data), we know that people in the higher income categories have higher incomes than those people in the lower categories, but we do not know exactly how much higher. Furthermore, two people with different income figures may belong to the same income group, which makes distinctions between the two impossible. In short, higher level data contain more information. The more information we have, the better statistical decisions we can make.

Having established that higher level measurement is preferred and that ratio or interval types of data should be collected if possible, the following question may immediately come into your mind: why does Question 7 in the above survey collect ordinal data (income groups) rather than ratio data (actual income figures)? You may also recall that most questionnaires you have encountered that solicit information about income collect the data in ordinal form. The choice of ordinal data collection here is out of consideration for the survey response rate (also called return rate). When response rate is low, we may not only have insufficient data points for statistical analysis, but also run into the problem of biased and unreliable data. Income is very sensitive personal information and most people are reluctant to release it. Therefore, they are less likely to respond to the survey or may respond to the survey without answering the income question if we ask their exact income amounts. In contrast, income expressed in a category is less sensitive and people are more likely to respond to the question. The same reasoning can be applied to questions about age. Therefore, while we prefer ratio data from a statistical standpoint, practical considerations may dictate that we collect the data using an ordinal scale.

CHAPTER 2

Avoiding Manual Calculations and Formula Manipulations— Using Software

Complicated mathematical formulae and lengthy manual calculation processes deterred many people from doing statistical analysis in the early days of the history of statistics. Even after statistical software packages for mainframe computers appeared in the late 1960s, statistical analysis still remained in the hands of a small group of academics and researchers who were comfortable with computers and had access to computing facilities. Statistical software for microcomputers emerged about 15 years ago. This development simplified statistical analysis to a great extent and also made statistical software more widely accessible. However, statistical software for the MS-DOS operating system typically required users to learn complicated syntax and file structures, which was still a hurdle for many people. Today, statistical software packages written for Windows or other graphical operating systems typically do not call for the use of any special syntax. Even an advanced statistical analysis now requires only a few mouse clicks, allowing us to completely avoid manual calculations and formula manipulations.

2.1 Types of Software

There is a variety of software on the market that can be used to perform statistical analysis. Different software have different capabilities and present results in different output formats. This book will demonstrate how to read and interpret results from the most recent versions (at the time of writing in early 2000) of two common Windows software packages: SPSS version 10 and Microsoft Excel 2000.[1] Each of these packages represents a different type of software. SPSS is the most popular statistical software used in social sciences. It is a specialized package designed specifically for statistical analysis of data. Excel is a spreadsheet software package that is normally purchased as part of the Microsoft Office suite of software. In addition to the financial and mathematical functions traditionally found in spreadsheet software, Excel has some statistical capabilities. However, since Excel is not a specialized statistical software package, it can only perform basic statistical analysis and is more difficult to use than true statistical software for some statistical tests. On the other hand, Excel's statistical component is still easier to use than those found in some other spreadsheet software. Excel's ability to produce graphs is superior to many statistical software packages and the graphs it generates can be easily imported into word processor documents, especially into Microsoft Word, which is another component of Microsoft Office.

Once you have learned how to read and interpret the output from one software package, it is very easy to switch to another because they all include similar information even though the output formats or notation may be different. This means that even if you are using software other than Excel or SPSS, you can still apply what you learn here to that software. Similarly, you can easily understand the output from earlier (or even later) versions of the same software once you have learned the versions used in this book.

2.2   Which Software to Select

With the advent of sophisticated statistical software for microcomputers, choosing between using mainframe and microcomputer systems is almost a non-issue today. Microcomputers and the statistical packages available for them are quite capable of handling complicated analyses of large data sets. Thus, the major decision is choosing between general-purpose spreadsheet software and specialized statistical software. Spreadsheet software can do most of the basic statistical analysis covered in this book while statistical software also provides more advanced functions beyond the basics. Therefore, if you only need basic statistical functions, there is no need to buy statistical software as long as your office suite includes good spreadsheet software that can do the job (e.g., Microsoft Office, which includes Excel). Statistical software is often much more expensive than spreadsheet software, sometimes costing over a thousand dollars. However, if you are in a large organization, such as a university, you may be able to buy a license for expensive statistical software at a much lower price under a site license or bulk licensing plan.

Once you make a choice between statistical software and spreadsheet software, it is very difficult for me to recommend a particular product because the market keeps changing. Major companies are all very competitive and bring out improved versions of their software packages on a regular basis. The best approach is to read software reviews and talk to users of various software in order to decide which product has your preferred features at the time you are making the purchasing decision. You should also consider other factors such as price, compatibility with your existing software for transferring files, and your familiarity with the company's other software (different products from the same company often have very consistent interfaces). It is usually not advisable to buy a small company's products because the company may go out of business, which would leave you with no technical support or new versions. A small company may also lack good technical support should you need it.

In addition to commercial software, there are now Web sites that allow you to submit your data and run statistical tests free of charge. You need to check out the reliability and authoritativeness of the Web site before you trust data analysis results obtained in this way.

2.3   How to Organize Data into a Computer File

If you are using software to do data analysis for the first time, the first question you will encounter is how to organize and input your data into the software. Although different software have very different user interfaces, they all follow the same basic structure for data input regardless of whether it is statistical or spreadsheet software: **Each column represents a variable and each row is a data point.** For example, if you have conducted a survey with 10 questions and 100 people responded to the survey, then you have 10 variables and 100 data points.[2] You can then create 10 columns with each column representing a question and 100 rows with each row representing a respondent's answers to the questions. You need to name the columns to indicate the meaning of the variables, e.g., gender. Figure 2-1 is a sample file in Excel with three variables (gender, age, and income) and four data points.

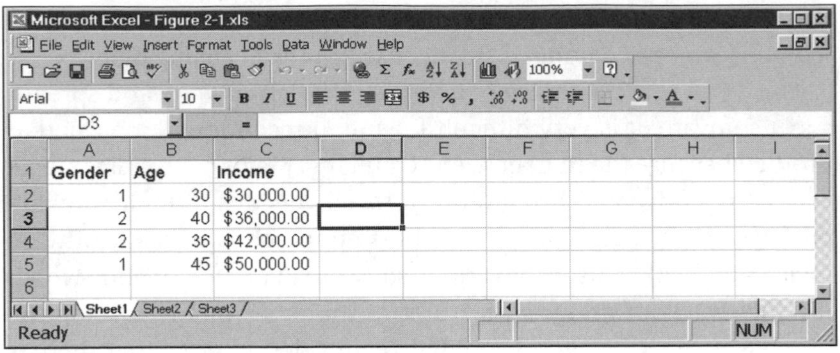

Figure 2-1 A Sample Excel Data File

If the data you collected are not in a numerical format, then you need to code the data before inputting them into the software. For example, you can code female as 1 and male as 2 for the gender variable as shown in Figure 2-1. The coding of ordinal data, such as poor, average, good, excellent, is not completely arbitrary. Please refer to Chapter 1, Sections 1.1 and 1.2 for discussions on coding nominal and ordinal data.

2.4 How to Deal with Missing Data

In most real data collection situations, you will encounter the missing data problem—the value of a particular variable for a particular data point is unknown. This problem can happen for various reasons. In a survey, a survey respondent may not answer one or more questions. In an experiment, a subject may drop out of the experiment halfway through, leaving data collection for that subject incomplete. It can also happen when a particular piece of information was obviously recorded incorrectly and you decide not to use it. When you collect data from a written record, such as a directory, the particular data you wanted may not be there. For example, a particular library or information center did not report their statistics for a particular year.

Different software have different ways of dealing with the missing data issue. Understanding how to declare missing data correctly in the software you are using is a very important step in ensuring the correctness of your data analysis results. Lack of this understanding can have terrible consequences for your results. Some software, such as Excel, do not have a built-in mechanism to deal with the missing data problem and you must come up with creative solutions yourself.

Statistical software usually do have some kind of built-in mechanism to deal with the missing data issue and require you to explicitly declare missing data. In SPSS, you declare missing data on the page that is shown when you click on the "Variable View" tab at the bottom of the "Data Editor" window (you also define other characteristics of the variable here, such as data type). For example, you can use "9999" to represent a missing data point for the age variable. The number 9999 is used because it is impossible to appear as a real value for age (nobody can be 9999 years old). Once you declare that 9999 represents missing data in the age variable, SPSS will then ignore 9999 in any calculations for this variable, such as calculating the average age. You can even have more than one value to represent missing data in the same variable. This allows you to code the reason for the data being missing. For age, 9999 may represent cases where no response was given, while 8888 represents cases where the value was obviously incorrect (e.g., an age of 2 when all respondents were known to be adults).

The number you choose to represent missing data must be a number that is impossible to appear as a real value for this variable. For instance, you cannot use 9999 to represent missing data for the salary variable because 9999 is a possible salary figure. This principle applies no matter what software you are using. Other than this restriction, you are free to choose whatever number you wish to represent missing data. For example, you can use a negative number to represent missing values for salary data since salary cannot be negative. You can also choose different numbers for different variables in the same data file. However, it is a good idea to use the same number to represent missing data for all the variables in the same file to avoid confusion.

As spreadsheet rather than statistical software, Excel does not have any built-in mechanism to deal with missing data. In other words, you cannot explicitly declare a number to represent missing data and expect Excel to ignore it in calculations. However, Excel will ignore empty cells in any calculations, so you can represent missing data by simply leaving the appropriate cells empty.

A common misunderstanding that I have observed among students in their first statistics course is to equate zero with missing data. Zero can be a real figure in variables such as income while missing data means that the income for the person is unknown and could be thousands of dollars for all we know. Missing data will not be used in any calculations while zero as a real figure contributes to all kinds of data analysis you perform on the variable. For example, the average of 3, 3, and 0 is 2 (3+3+0 = 6; to get the average divide 6 by 3 data points, which gives an average of 2), while the average of 3, 3, and a missing data point is 3 (3+3 = 6; to get the average divide 6 by 2 data points, which gives an average of 3).

Recent versions of various software packages all include the ability to import and export files for other software packages as well as "generic" file formats accessible by most software (e.g., text files). For instance, you can easily export data from SPSS to an Excel file and then load it into Excel to do data analysis. You can also import an Excel file into SPSS to perform analysis that cannot be done in Excel. **Great care must be taken in doing data transfers if you have missing data**. For example, you may have declared in SPSS that 9999 represents missing data for the variable "Age." When you save the data to an Excel file and then load it into Excel, 9999 will not be recognized as missing data by Excel, since it has no built-in mechanism for dealing with missing data. The average age calculated by Excel will be inflated by a single 9999 figure and you may not even be aware of the error![3]

Endnotes

1. SPSS for Windows is copyright 1989-1999 by SPSS, Inc. Microsoft Excel is copyright 1985-1999 by Microsoft Corp.

2. Most survey questions correspond to a variable. However, there are exceptions; e.g., you allow respondents to choose more than one answer to a specific question. How you deal with this situation in data input depends on how you want to analyze the data. If you have open-ended questions such as asking people to verbally express their opinion on an issue, you cannot input these data into statistical software.

3. In this situation, you can use the Find and Replace function in Excel to locate and clear these "9999" codes before you start working with the imported data. This will replace them with empty cells, the correct way to handle missing data in Excel as discussed above.

CHAPTER 3

First Look—Using Graphs to See the Characteristics of Data

It has been said that a picture is worth a thousand words. The value of a picture or a graph in representing data may not be as well known, but is as great or even greater. To describe the value of graphs in presenting data, I would say that a graph is worth a thousand data points. When a thousand data points are presented in raw form, it is very difficult, if not impossible, to see a pattern or trend. However, when these data points are summarized into a proper graph, we not only gain an immediate visual impression of its pattern, but may also see a trend very quickly and easily. In short, graphs can often convey messages in the data very effectively.

Using computer software to do statistical analysis has not only liberated us from complicated mathematical formulae and lengthy calculations, but also freed us from the tedious tabulations needed to generate tables or graphs. All statistical and spreadsheet software have the capability to produce graphs from data. With Windows software, such as Excel, you can often produce a wide range of professional graphs with a few mouse clicks. You can also easily experiment with the effects of different types or dimensions of the graph.

3.1 Variety of Graphs

There are various kinds of graphs. I will use some of the data collected in the 1996 Canadian federal depository library survey (Dolan and Vaughan, 1998) to illustrate how different types of graphs can be used for different purposes. The purpose of the survey was to investigate whether Canadian depository libraries are prepared for the transition to electronic delivery of government information. One of the questions asked in the survey was the type of computer operating system used in public service PCs (a public service PC is a PC used by the library patrons rather than the staff). Table 3-1 shows the percentage of different operating systems in all the libraries surveyed.

Table 3-1   Percentage of Different Operating Systems

Operating System	All Depository Libraries	Academic Library	Public Library	Government Library
MS-DOS	20.0%	18.56%	23.98%	11.16%
Windows 3.1	40.8%	40.61%	39.55%	57.02%
Windows 95	25.2%	25.92%	24.55%	14.46%
Windows NT	3.1%	0.63%	7.68%	11.98%
Other	10.9%	14.28%	4.25%	5.37%

Originally, there were thousands of data points for this survey question (each of the 450 libraries participating in the survey reported the number of PCs with these five different operating systems). It would be impossible to make sense of these thousands of data points if they were presented directly. However, it becomes easier to digest the information once the data are summarized into a table. Some people may still have difficulty visualizing the pattern of data when it is presented in a table form. Graphs, on the other hand, will convey the information better. For example, Figure 3-1 presents the data in the second column of Table 3-1 in a bar graph. The graph gives us a clearer sense of how different operating systems are distributed in all depository libraries.

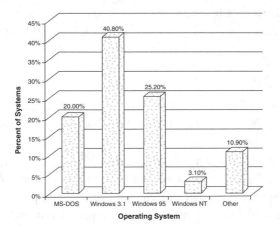

Figure 3-1   Percentage of Operating Systems for All Depository Libraries

It is immediately obvious that Windows 3.1 is the most common operating system and Windows NT the least common one. In any bar graph where some bars are almost too low to be visible, such as the bar for Windows NT in Figure 3-1, it is always a good idea to label the bars with their values as demonstrated in Figure 3-1. You may have seen bar graphs in the form of Figure 3-2, which is essentially Figure 3-1 rotated by 90 degrees. The two graphs contain exactly the same information and the choice of which one to use is a matter of preference.

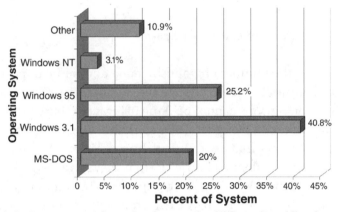

Figure 3-2   Percentage of Operating Systems for All Depository Libraries

Another way of presenting the data in the second column of Table 3-1 is by a pie chart as demonstrated in Figure 3-3. The pie chart contains the same information as the bar graph. However, the pie chart has the advantage of allowing us to highlight a particular category by exploding a slice of the pie (move a section of the pie chart slightly outward). This is particularly useful if you want to call attention to a particular category to make a point. For instance, I exploded the MS-DOS slice in Figure 3-3 to emphasize that one-fifth of the computers are equipped with MS-DOS which is incapable of accessing government information on the World Wide Web via a graphical interface.

There are different types of depository libraries, including public libraries, academic libraries, government libraries, and others. The last three columns of Table 3-1 show the distribution of operating systems in three different types of libraries. If you use pie charts to present these data you need three charts, one for each type of library. If you use a bar graph, however, you only need one graph as shown in Figure 3-4. Presenting the three different types of libraries in the same

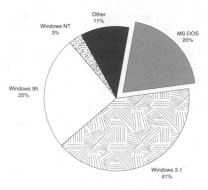

Figure 3-3   MS-DOS vs. Other Operating Systems

graph reduces the number of graphs needed and, more importantly, makes the contrast between different types of libraries easily discernable. Such comparisons cannot be done using a pie chart. This shows the disadvantage of a pie chart when compared to a bar graph.

Figure 3-4 shows that government libraries are better equipped than public and academic libraries in that they have fewer MS-DOS computers and more Windows 3.1 computers. The same comparison can be made by another type of bar graph, the stacked bar graph demonstrated in Figure 3-5. The bottom section of the bars in Figure 3-5 stands for MS-DOS and the next section up is Windows 3.1. The contrast between government libraries and the other types of libraries in these two sections are very strong. Figure 3-4 and Figure 3-5 are based on the same data and convey the same information. To

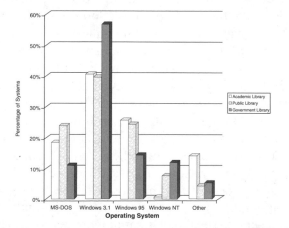

Figure 3-4   A Comparison of Operating Systems in Different Types of Libraries

some people, the breakdown of different operating systems in each type of library is clearer in Figure 3-5. The choice between Figure 3-4 and Figure 3-5 is, again, a matter of familiarity and preference.

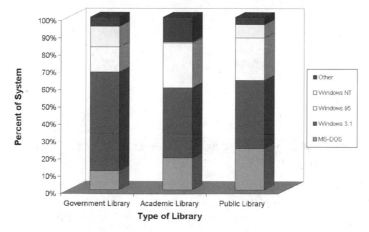

Figure 3-5   A Comparison of Operating Systems in Different Types of Libraries

The above graphs have only one variable, the type of operating system. Pie charts and bar graphs are suitable in this circumstance. In many other situations, however, we need to plot two variables on the same graph in order to show the relationship between them or to investigate the effect of one variable on the other. Line charts can be used for this purpose. A good example in information science is the recall-precision graph often seen in information retrieval literature. Suppose that you collected recall and precision data in an information retrieval experiment as shown in Table 3-2. Plotting these data in a line chart results in Figure 3-6. Each pair of data in Table 3-2 (the pairs are obtained by reading down each column) is represented by a dot in Figure 3-6. Connecting these 10 dots we get a downward trend line. The line chart clearly shows the inverse relationship between recall and precision: as recall increases, precision decreases. A glance at the data in Table 3-2 will not give us as clear an image of the relationship as the line chart does.

Table 3-2   Recall and Precision Data

Recall	0.15	0.20	0.23	0.27	0.30	0.35	0.40	0.45	0.55	0.60
Precision	0.70	0.65	0.60	0.50	0.48	0.40	0.36	0.30	0.28	0.20

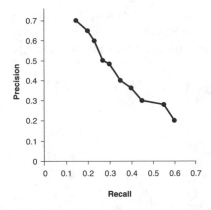

Figure 3-6 Relationship Between Recall and Precision

The advantage of a line chart is even more obvious if you collect recall-precision data for two different retrieval systems and intend to make a comparison. Figure 3-7 contains recall-precision lines for two hypothetical information retrieval systems. A quick look at Figure 3-7 tells us that System B is better than System A because the former lies higher than the latter. This means that for a given recall value, System B has a higher precision value than System A.

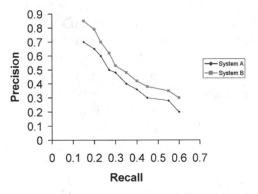

Figure 3-7 Recall and Precision of Two Information Retrieval Systems

3.2 A Special Bar Graph—Histogram

There is not much need to explain how to read common graphs such as those presented in the previous section because they are relatively familiar to us. However, the most important type of graph in statistical analysis, the histogram, is not familiar to most people and warrants a special discussion here. A histogram is a bar graph for the frequency distribution of a group of data. You may wonder what is a frequency distribution. To explain this new concept, suppose that we collected data on respondents' ages in a survey and the data are as shown in Figure 3-8.

22, 23, 26, 27, 28, 31, 32, 33, 33, 34, 35, 36, 37, 37, 38, 39, 40, 40, 41, 41,
42, 42, 43, 44, 44, 45, 45, 45, 46, 47, 47, 47, 49, 49, 50, 50, 51, 51, 52, 53,
54, 55, 55, 56, 57, 58, 61, 62, 63, 67.

Figure 3-8 Age Data from a Survey

Looking at this pile of raw data, it is hard to get a grip on what we can learn from the data and what pattern the data may have. To make sense of any data set, we can first organize the data into groups and then count the number of data points in each group. For instance, we can set up age groups as shown in the left column of Table 3-3 and then record the number of people in each age group as shown in the right column of the table. The resulting table is the frequency distribution of the age variable.

Table 3-3 Frequency Distribution of Age Variable

Age Group	Number of people in this age group
17.5 – 22.5	1
22.5 – 27.5	3
27.5 – 32.5	3
32.5 – 37.5	7
37.5 – 42.5	8
42.5 – 47.5	10
47.5 – 52.5	7
52.5 – 57.5	6
57.5 – 62.5	3
62.5 – 67.5	2

Table 3-3 indicates how many data points fall into each group, which can also be described as the frequency with which data points are distributed across the different groups, hence the term frequency distribution. It provides us with a first look at the underlying pattern of the data set. To gain a graphical sense of this pattern, we can plot this table into a two-dimensional bar graph as shown in Figure 3-9. In the Figure, the age groups are on the X-axis (horizontal axis) and the number of people in each age group is indicated on the Y-axis (vertical axis). This bar graph is the histogram of the age variable. All the tedious work of counting the number of people in each group and then plotting it as a histogram can be done in seconds by any software that has some statistical functions. In fact, Table 3-3 was generated by SPSS software with a few mouse clicks (selecting menu options "Analyze," "Descriptive Statistics," "Frequencies," etc.). The software also decided the age groups automatically, which explains why there are decimal points in the grouping.

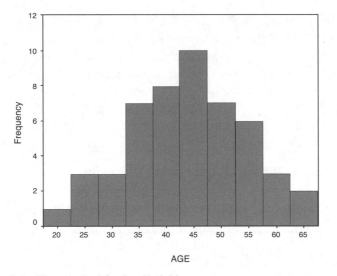

Figure 3-9   Histogram of the Age Variable

The histogram of the age variable in Figure 3-9 gives us a better idea of the age distribution than the numbers in Table 3-3 alone. The height of the bar for each age group indicates the frequency of the data points falling within that age group. That is, the higher the bar for a particular age group, the more people belong to that group. We can use the histogram to see if any age group is more common than any other age group.

It should be emphasized that a histogram involves only one variable. In a histogram, the X-axis always represents the variable being graphed. The Y-axis always indicates the number of data points falling within a given group, i.e., the frequency with which data points fall into the group. In contrast, many two-dimensional graphs we see in daily life have two variables each represented by X and Y-axes. For example, Figure 3-10 shows the relationship between age and income where the X-axis represents the age variable and the Y-axis the income variable. Figure 3-9 and Figure 3-10 are different types of graphs designed for different purposes. Both are valid but each conveys very different information to us. Figure 3-9 tells us that the survey respondents' ages are distributed in the following pattern: more people are in the middle age range, fewer people are in the high or low end of the age groups. Figure 3-10 shows us that income increases as age increases until about age 65 and then decreases. The recall-precision chart in Figure 3-6 is another example of a two-variable graph.

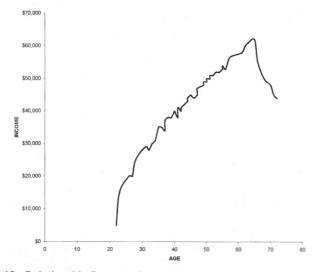

Figure 3-10   Relationship Between Age and Income

To summarize, a histogram is a bar graph for the frequency distribution of the data. A frequency distribution can also be represented by other types of graphs, such as the "stem-and-leaf" graph. This book introduces only the histogram, which is the most common type, and uses the terms "frequency distribution" and "histogram" almost interchangeably for convenience of discussion. Frequency distributions like the one shown in Figure 3-9 are called symmetrical or unskewed distributions (it is not a perfect symmetrical distribution, which rarely exists). In fact, it can be said to resemble the normal distribution—a specific kind of perfectly symmetrical distribution that has a bell shape. The normal distribution has many unique characteristics that will be discussed in Chapter 5, Section 5.5.

Not all frequency distributions are symmetrical. There are many unsymmetrical or skewed distributions. Income data usually have a skewed distribution as shown in Figure 3-11. A symmetrical distribution typically peaks around the middle of the histogram while a skewed distribution peaks at right or left end. The histogram in Figure 3-11 can be interpreted to mean that very few people have very high incomes while the majority of people have low or moderate incomes, a phenomenon of wealth distribution in our society. Many other variables, such as the population served by public libraries and funding of these libraries, also have skewed distributions. This is because very few libraries serve very large populations and receive large amounts of funding while more libraries serve medium to small populations and receive proportionately smaller amounts of funding.

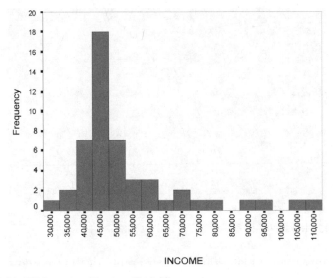

Figure 3-11   Histogram of Income Variable

A histogram gives a graphical summary of the nature of the data set. The shape of the frequency distribution, i.e., skewed or symmetrical, will be a factor in deciding the type of statistical analysis that we can use. For this reason, the discussion of the histogram in this chapter paves the way for subsequent chapters in which we will discuss various types of statistical methods.

CHAPTER 4

Summarizing Messy Data into Neat Figures—Descriptive Statistics

The histograms discussed in the previous chapter organized a pile of data, such as the age data in Figure 3-8, into graphical forms, such as Figure 3-9. The histograms give us a sense of how the data are distributed and what characteristics they have. This is just one of the ways we can describe and summarize data. There are other methods too. For example, if someone asks you to describe the age data you collected, you would not reply by reading all the numbers to the person. Nor would you go and fetch the histogram to answer the question. Most likely you would simply say that the ages range from 22 to 67 years old with an average of 44. Although you may not be aware of it, what you have done here is exactly what descriptive statistics do—summarize a pile of messy data into a few neat figures. The "average" (44) is one of the measures of central tendency and the "range" (from 22 to 67) is one of the measures of variability. What I will do in this chapter is to introduce a few new measurements based on these familiar ones and discuss when it is appropriate to use a particular measurement.

4.1 Measures of Central Tendency

Central tendency is the tendency of the data points to center on a particular value that is representative of the data set. Measures of central tendency show us the center of the data set. The meaning of central tendency may still be vague now but will be clearer after we examine the three measures of central tendency: mean, median, and mode. These three measures are suitable for different data types and data with different frequency distributions.

4.1.1   Mean—The Arithmetic Average

The mean, a statistical term, is exactly equivalent to the arithmetic average that we are all familiar with in daily life. The mean, or arithmetic average, is calculated by adding up all the data points, then dividing by the number of data points. For example, the mean of 20 and 40 is calculated as (20+40)/2, which is 30. We can convert this calculation into a more generic form by letting X_1 represent the value of data point 1, and X_2 represent the value of data point 2, so that the average of the two values will be $(X_1 + X_2)/2$. If there are ten data points, we will add from X_1 to X_{10} and then divide by 10. In mathematics, a succinct way of expressing adding from X_1 to X_{10} is $\sum_{i=1}^{n} x_i$. Therefore, the formula to calculate the mean for any number of data points is:

$$\bar{x} = \frac{\sum_{i=1}^{n} x_i}{n}$$

where $\bar{x}$ stands for the mean and n represents the number of data points. This formula tells us to add up all the data points from X_1 to X_n and then divide by the number of data points (n), which is exactly how we said we should calculate the mean at the beginning of this section. I promise that Σ (pronounced as "sigma") is the only mathematical symbol that you will have to deal with in this statistics book. I introduce it here because your understanding of how to calculate the mean may help you understand Σ. If you still do not understand the meaning of Σ, do not worry. Since your computer will do the calculations for you, you do not really need to remember and understand formulae perfectly. The focus of this book is on understanding the logic and the meaning of statistical methods without the usual hurdles presented by mathematical formulae.

The interpretation of the mean or average is clear to all of us. It summarizes a data set by a single figure and allows us to make comparisons between different data sets. For instance, if there are two groups of people, one with an average age of 30 and the other with an average age of 40, we know that people in the first group are, on average, younger than people in the second group.

Why do we need other measures of central tendency when the mean is so simple and easy to understand? The answer is that the mean can give us a distorted impression of the data in some situations. To illustrate, suppose that you are studying the income of information consultants and have collected annual income data from 50 consultants as shown in Figure 4-1.

$30,000	$33,000	$35,000	$38,000	$38,500	$39,000	$39,000	$40,000
$41,500	$42,000	$42,500	$43,000	$43,000	$43,500	$43,600	$43,800
$44,000	$44,000	$44,000	$44,200	$44,300	$44,500	$45,000	$45,000
$45,000	*$45,600*	$46,300	$47,000	$49,000	$50,000	$50,000	$50,000
$50,000	$51,000	$52,000	$54,000	$55,000	$55,000	$58,000	$59,000
$60,000	$65,000	$69,000	$70,000	$75,000	$80,000	$90,000	$95,000
$105,000	$110,000						

Figure 4-1   Income Data of 50 Information Consultants

The mean of these 50 data points is calculated at $52,526. You may conclude that the average annual income of these information consultants is around $52,500. However, a closer look at the data reveals that most of the consultants have an income that is below this average figure. The reason that the average turns out to be so high is that the incomes from a few consultants earning over $80,000 inflate the average figure. In this case, if you use the mean as the measure of central tendency, you will get a wrong impression of incomes for this group of people. If we plot these income data in a histogram as shown in Figure 4-2, we can get a better understanding of the problem.

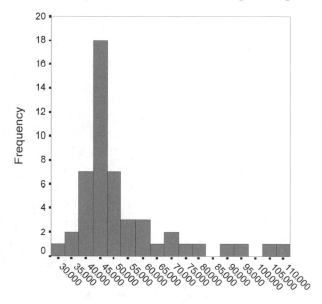

INCOME

Figure 4-2   Histogram of Information Consultants' Income

The histogram shows a skewed distribution of incomes. Most people's incomes are at the low end of the histogram (left side) while only a few people are at the high end (right side). The few high-end income data pull the mean away from the center of the distribution. This is not an isolated case of distortion. In fact, a skewed distribution always pulls the mean away from the center either toward the high end or the low end depending on the direction of the skewness. Therefore, the mean is not an appropriate measure of central tendency for data with a skewed frequency distribution. The median, another measure of central tendency, should be used in this situation.

4.1.2   Median—The Middle Point

The median is the exact middle point of the frequency distribution. To calculate the median, we first sort the data set either from low to high, as in Figure 4-1, or high to low. If there are an odd number of data points, the median is the value of the middle score. For example, the median for the data set 3, 5, 9, 11, 14 is 9. If there are an even number of data points, then the median is the average of the two middle scores. For example, the median for the data set 3, 5, 9, 11, 14, 18 is 10 (the average of 9 and 11). It is clear from the way median is calculated that 50 percent of the data points lie above the median and the other 50 percent lie below it. Thus the statistical term median has exactly the same meaning as the median strip on a street that has half of the street on its left side and the other half on its right side.

For the data set in Figure 4-1 the median is $45,300 (the average of $45,000 and $45,600, the two highlighted numbers in Figure 4-1). This means that a typical information consultant's income is $45,300. The extreme data points do not affect the median as they do the mean. As can be seen from Figure 4-2, the median of $45,300 locates at the center of the distribution while the mean of $52,526 does not. More data points fall around the median of $45,300 than around the mean of $52,526. So the median is more representative of the data set and its central point. To summarize, the mean is an appropriate measure of central tendency for interval and ratio data if the distribution is not skewed. If the distribution is skewed, then median should be used.

The median is also used as the measure of central tendency for ordinal data regardless of whether the frequency distribution is skewed or not. The calculation of the median for ordinal data is the same as for interval or ratio data. Suppose we asked users to rate the overall effectiveness of a new retrieval system using a five-point scale of poor, fair, satisfactory, good, and excellent and got the following data:

1, 2, 2, 3, 3, 3, 3, 4, 4, 4, 4, 4, 5, 5, 5, 5, 5

where 1 stands for poor and 5 for excellent. The median will be 4, which tells us that a typical user rated the system as good.

The reason that the mean cannot be used for ordinal data will be clear if we recall the definition and the nature of ordinal data (see Chapter 1, Section 1.2). For the rating data above, we know that 4 is a better rating than 3, which in turn is better than 2, but we cannot say that the difference between 1 and 2 is equal to that between 3 and 4. The calculation of the mean, however, mathematically assumes that the differences are the same.

4.1.3 Mode—The Peak of the Histogram

Why do we want to introduce yet another measure of central tendency after mean and median? Because neither mean nor median can be applied to nominal data. Imagine that we have collected data on gender in a survey and coded male as 1 and female as 2. If we then calculate the average of these 1s and 2s, we would find it to be something between 1 and 2, say 1.5. What does this 1.5 mean? Does it mean that the average person in the survey is someone who is half male and half female? The same problem will occur if we use median as the measure of central tendency here.

Mode is the only appropriate measure of central tendency for nominal data. The mode is the most frequently occurring score in a distribution. In a histogram, the mode is always located beneath the tallest bar (Sprinthall, 1997, 36). In other words, the peak of a histogram signals the mode. For nominal data, we do not have to graph the data to determine the mode. By definition of the mode, we just have to decide which category occurs most frequently, or which value of the code is most common. For example, a 1996 survey of Canadian federal depository libraries found that the distribution of different Web browsers on public service PCs were as shown in Table 4-1 (Dolan and Vaughan, 1998, 30).

If we code the four Web browsers from 1 to 4 according to the sequence they are listed in the table, then the mode is 2, meaning that Netscape was the most common Web browser at the time of the survey. For nominal data, other than reporting the mode, it is always a good idea to report the frequencies and even the percentages for all the categories as shown in Table 4-1 to provide a better description of the data.

In addition to being the only measure of central tendency for nominal data, mode is also the measure of central tendency for any

Table 4-1 Web Browser Distribution

Browser	Number of Installations	Percentage
Internet Explorer	338	5.25%
Netscape	5455	84.80%
Text Browser	637	9.9%
Other	3	0.05%
TOTAL	**6433**	**100.00%**

other type of data when the distribution is bimodal or multi-modal. Bimodal means that the frequency distribution has two modes or peaks and multi-modal means that the distribution has three or more modes. To give an example of a bimodal distribution, suppose that we surveyed a group of people on their attitude toward introducing a fee for service in public libraries. We measured their attitude by a series of questions and then summarized their answers

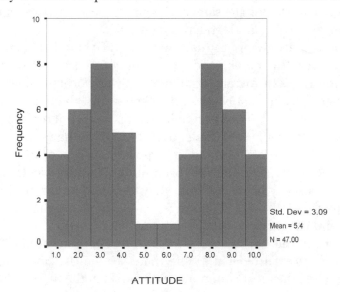

Figure 4-3 Example of a Bimodal Distribution

into an attitude score ranging from 1 (strongly anti) to 10 (strongly pro) with 5 and 6 being relatively neutral. If there is a strong split on the issue among people being surveyed, the frequency distribution of the attitude score may look like the one shown in Figure 4-3.

Both the mean and the median are 5 (neutral), which does not at all reflect the opinion of most people. Apparently, a bimodal distribution cannot be adequately described by a single central tendency figure. In this case, we should report both modes, 3 (anti) and 8 (pro), as central tendency to provide an accurate account of the situation. This means that people are typically either anti or pro on the issue rather than being neutral.

4.1.4 When to Use Which Measure of Central Tendency —A Summary

Having discussed the three central tendency measures and the factors that should be considered in the choice of a measure, it is now the time for a summary to provide a clear overall picture. There are two factors in the decision of which measure to use: shape of the frequency distribution and the type of data. If the distribution is bimodal or multi-modal, only mode can be used and all the modes should be reported to describe the data. If the distribution is unimodal (one peak), then consider the type of data. For nominal data, use mode; for ordinal data, use median. For interval and ratio data, we have to look at the frequency distribution again. If the distribution is skewed, use median. If the distribution is approximately symmetrical, use mean. Figure 4-4 is a chart summarizing this decision process.

It should be pointed out that for unimodal interval and ratio data, mean should be used unless the distribution is badly skewed. In other words, a little skewness does not call for the use of median. In fact, real data sets very rarely have a perfectly symmetrical distribution. You may still wonder how skewed is skewed enough to warrant the use of median. To answer this question, let us look at two real frequency distributions in information science. A sample of 50 Ontario public libraries was taken and data for two variables were collected from Ontario library statistics for those libraries: collection size (number of collection items) and collection size per capita (collection size divided by the population of the service area). Figure 4-5 and Figure 4-6 are the frequency distributions for these two data sets.

Figure 4-5 represents a badly skewed distribution and the median should be used as the measure of central tendency. The mean of

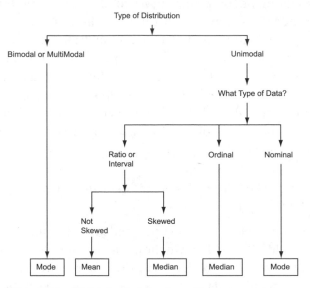

Figure 4-4   When to Use Which Central Tendency Measure

138,551 is inflated by the huge collection size a few large libraries had. The median of 80,320 is a better representation of a typical library's collection size. Figure 4-6 is an approximately symmetrical distribution although it is also a little skewed. This amount of skewness does not call for the use of median. In fact, the mean of 3.2 is very close to the median of 2.9, which is true for all the distributions that are not very skewed. In the case of Figure 4-5 the mean and the median are very far part (138,551 versus 80,320). Thus, a large discrepancy between the mean and the median is also a sign that the distribution is skewed enough to justify the use of median as the measure of central tendency.

Figure 4-6 is not perfectly unimodal in the sense there are some little fluctuations in the histogram. These little fluctuations should not be taken to mean that the distribution is bimodal or multi-modal. Perfectly smooth distribution is extremely rare in real life. Unless there are two or more very pronounced modes as shown in Figure 4-3, we usually treat the distribution as unimodal.

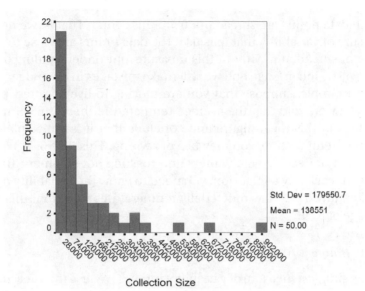

Figure 4-5   Frequency Distribution of Collection Size

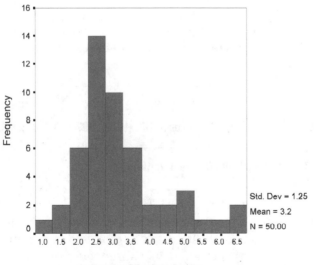

Figure 4-6   Frequency Distribution of Collection Size Per Capita

4.2   Measures of Variability

Once we have a measure of central tendency to indicate the center of the distribution, we need a measurement to indicate the extent to which data points are spread out from this center. That is, we need a measure of variability that tells us if the data points are close to each other or spread out. Without this measure, our understanding of the data will be incomplete and we will make mistakes in our judgement. As an example, suppose that you are moving to live in a new place and you were told that the average temperature there is 65°F. If you just look at this mean figure and conclude that it is a nice place in terms of temperature, you may be very wrong. This nice 65°F can be the result of freezing cold winters and roasting hot summers. Before you can reach any conclusion, you need to know the variability of the temperatures, i.e., how much daily temperatures vary from this nice average of 65°F.

4.2.1 Range

The simplest measure of variability is range. We use this measure in our daily life all the time: the temperature varies from 30°F to 100°F; the salary varies from $20,000 to $100,000. The calculation of range is very simple; it is the difference between the highest value and the lowest value in a data set. Although range is very easy to calculate and understand, it is not commonly used in statistics because it has some problems. To illustrate, consider the two data sets in Figure 4-7.

Data Set A:	**0, 60, 61, 62, 62, 63, 63, 64, 64, 66, 67, 100**
Data Set B:	**0, 0, 0, 0, 66, 66, 100, 100, 100, 100, 100, 100**

Figure 4-7 Two Data Sets with Different Variability

Both data sets have a mean of 61. However, data set A has less variability. All the data points are fairly close to the mean of 61 other than the two extreme data points. If the two sets of data represent samples of daily temperatures measured in Fahrenheit from two different places, we would say that place A is better than place B. On most days, place A would have comfortable temperatures of around 63°F while most days in place B are either too hot or too cold. However, if we measure the variability by range, then the two data sets will get the same result, a range of 100. This illustrates the first problem with the range: it only takes two extreme data points into consideration. If the last number in data set A is a typo in data collection and it should be

67, then the range of 100 is a badly exaggerated measure of variability. This illustrates another problem of using range as the measure of variability: it can be very sensitive to a single error in data collection.

4.2.2 Interquartile Range (IQR)

Interquartile range (IQR) as a measure of variability is designed to be resistant to the effect of extreme data points. This resistance is obvious from the way that IQR is calculated: sort the data points from low to high or high to low and then ignore the top and bottom 25 percent of the data points. The range of the remaining 50 percent of the data points is the interquartile range. In other words, divide the sorted data into four quarters and disregard the top quarter and the bottom quarter of the data. Then calculate the difference between the largest and the smallest numbers in remaining data to get IQR. For data set A in Figure 4-7, the IQR is 2 (64–62). For data set B it is 100 (100–0), indicating a greater variability. Unlike the range, which shows no difference between data set A and B in terms of variability, the interquartile range distinguishes the two data sets better. However, the calculation of IQR still involves only a few data points. In contrast, standard deviation, another measure of variability discussed in the next section, includes all of the data points in its calculation.

4.2.3 Standard Deviation (SD)

Standard deviation (SD for short) is probably the most commonly used measure of variability, so that even people who have not studied statistics have probably heard of it. However, its meaning may not be entirely clear, even to those who have been exposed to some beginning statistics. The formula to calculate standard deviation may look a little ugly to people who do not like math, but let us rely once again on computer software to do the calculation and focus our energy on the meaning instead. To make things simple, let us work with only four data points:

$$2, 4, 6, 8$$

The mean of these four data points is 5. To measure the variability of these data points from this mean of 5, we can calculate the difference between each data point and the mean as (2-5), (4-5), (6-5), and (8-5). This will result in the **deviation from the mean:** -3, -1, 1, 3.

To know the average deviation, we cannot simply calculate the arithmetic average of these four deviation figures because they will sum (add up) to zero. To avoid the problem of summing to zero, we need to cancel the negative signs in front of the first two deviation figures. This can be accomplished by squaring each of the four figures (i.e., multiplying each figure by itself), which will result in the **squared deviations from the mean**: 9, 1, 1, 9. The **average squared deviations from the mean** will be $(9+1+1+9)/4 = 5$.

If you look at the original four deviation figures (-3, -1, 1, 3) you will find that 5 is an exaggerated average deviation. If the largest deviation from the mean is 3, how can the average deviation be larger than that? This "exaggeration" results from applying the "square" operation to the deviation figures. We can cancel out this square effect by applying the "square root" operation to obtain the **average deviation from the mean**: $\sqrt{(9 + 1 + 1 + 9) / 4} = \sqrt{5} = 2.24$. Notice that the word "squared" is omitted from the verbal description here because the squared effect is cancelled out by the square root.

This figure of 2.24 more realistically represents the average deviation because it is between 1 and 3, the original deviation figures. This figure of 2.24 is called the standard deviation. The above calculation process shows that the standard deviation can be viewed as the average distance of data points from the mean. Thus, **standard deviation measures the variability or the degree of dispersion of the data set**.

The above standard deviation calculation process can be summarized into the formula:

$$SD = \sqrt{\frac{\sum\limits_{i=1}^{N} (x_i - \bar{x})^2}{N}}$$

where $\bar{x}$ stands for the mean and Σ stands for summation as discussed in Section 4.1.1 of this chapter. N is the number of data points. Using this formula, we can calculate standard deviations for the two data sets in Figure 4-7. The results are 22 for data set A and 47 for data set B. The smaller standard deviation for data set A indicates that there is less variability in that data set. Recall that the range as a measure of variability failed to distinguish between the two data sets, so the standard deviation is a better measure of variability in this case.

If you are not comfortable with the standard deviation formula, do not worry about it or struggle with it. You can use computer software to do all the calculations as will be shown later in this chapter (Section 4.3). You may also skip the following discussion about N vs. N-1 in the SD formula if you are not interested in mathematical complexities. Just focus on understanding the meaning of standard deviation and interpreting it correctly. Section 4.3 of this chapter will further elaborate on the meaning of standard deviation by tying it in with the measures of central tendency.

In the above standard deviation formula, I used N in the denominator for convenience of discussion (we added up N data points' deviation figures so we shall divide by N to get an average deviation figure). You may have seen that some books use N-1 instead of N in calculating standard deviation (Agresti and Finlay, 1997, 58). Because different books use different formulae (e.g., Sprinthall, 1997, 51, used N) there is a great confusion among many people as to which formula to use. Standard deviation is a difficult concept for many beginners already and this confusion certainly does not help alleviate this sense of difficulty.

The truth is that both formulae are correct, but are used in different situations. N is used in calculating population standard deviation and N-1 is used in sample standard deviation (Walsh, 1990, 44). "Population" and "sample" are two important terms in inferential statistics that will be discussed later in Chapter 5, Section 5.2. There is a technical reason for using N-1 for sample standard deviation and a detailed discussion is beyond the scope of this book. Interested readers can refer to (Walsh, 1990, 44–45) or (Sprinthall, 1997, 157–160). The good news about this confusion is that we do not have to be too concerned about when to use which formula. The chances are you will never calculate standard deviation manually and thus be confronted with the choice of formula. Most likely, you are going to use computer software to perform all the calculations and the software will take care of this problem. Besides, the calculation results from the two formulae will be very close anyway if N is fairly large (50 or greater), so there is really no need to worry about the choice of formula.

4.2.4 Variance

Variance is defined as the square of standard deviation, i.e., variance = SD^2. If SD = 4, then variance is 16. Variance is rarely used in descriptive statistics as a measure of variability. However, it is an important concept for a statistical test called analysis of variance, the topic of Chapter 10.

4.2.5 When to Use Which Measure of Variability
—A Summary

For interval or ratio data, standard deviation is the most appropriate measure of variability. However, if the frequency distribution of the data set is badly skewed, then interquartile range is preferred. This is because the standard deviation calculation is based on the mean, an inappropriate measure of central tendency for badly skewed distributions. Similarly, the interquartile range should be used instead of the standard deviation for ordinal data, since the mean does not apply to this type of data. As a general rule, when the median is being used as the appropriate measure of central tendency, the interquartile range is then typically reported as its measure of variability (Sprinthall, 1997, 49). The range may be used informally for a quick and easy measure of variability but it is not usually used in formal data analysis mainly because of its sensitivity to extreme data points. Variance is not usually used to describe the variability of a data set. It is used in the analysis of a variance test that will be discussed in Chapter 10.

4.3 Tying Together Descriptive Statistics Measures
—Examples

Now that we have discussed different measures of descriptive statistics, I am going to use an example to illustrate how to tie these different measures together to get a complete picture of the data. Being able to make sense of data in this way is the most important ability in data analysis when all the number crunching and calculations are done by a computer. The data I will use in this example come from the 1994 Ontario public library statistics for libraries serving populations between 5,000 to 500,000. Three variables are selected for analysis: the population of the service area, collection size as measured by the number of items in the collection, and collection size per capita. The third variable is the result of dividing the second variable by the first one. Excel 2000 will be used to carry out statistical analysis for this example.

To obtain descriptive statistics in Excel 2000, just go through the menu options: "Tools," "Data Analysis," and "Descriptive Statistics." Then provide information requested in the popup screen such as input range (where data are located) and output range (where statistical results should be displayed). The Excel output for all three variables are as shown in Figure 4-8.

	Population	Collection Size	Collection Size Per Capita
Mean	44989.2	120836.2	3.050031
Standard Error	5118.46	13829.15	0.089425
Median	17594.5	55907.5	2.841109
Mode	#N/A	#N/A	#N/A
Standard Deviation	67127.97	181367.6	1.1728
Sample Variance	4.51E+09	3.29E+10	1.375459
Kurtosis	14.76971	19.50418	1.045424
Skewness	3.442331	3.942646	0.770986
Range	475110	1369058	7.335617
Minimum	5060	1648	0.287709
Maximum	480170	1370706	7.623326
Sum	7738143	20783829	524.6053
Count	172	172	172
Largest(44)	50978	132924	3.727134
Smallest(44)	9871	32025	2.211649

Figure 4-8   Descriptive Statistics Output from Excel 2000

The histograms for the three variables are displayed in Figure 4-9 through Figure 4-11. Now that the computer has done all the calculations, we have to interpret the computer output. How would you interpret them? Which measure of central tendency and variability will you use? What do these measures tell us about the libraries? I suggest that you pause here for a few minutes and think about these questions. Then you can check your answers with the discussion below.

Excel does not know what kind of data are being analyzed so it calculates various measures of central tendency and variability. (Mode is shown as "#N/A," not applicable, because there is no single value that appeared more frequently than others.) It is up to you to decide which measures are appropriate. Recall that we summarized the process for determining the appropriate measure of central tendency into a chart in Figure 4-4. According to the chart, the first factor

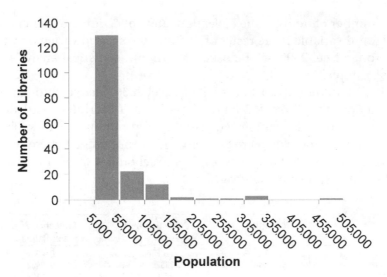

Figure 4-9 Histogram for "Population"

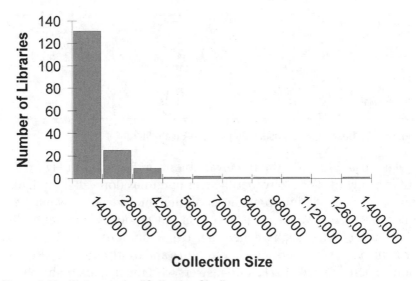

Figure 4-10 Histogram for "Collection Size"

we have to consider is the shape of the frequency distribution. All three histograms are unimodal. So the next factor to consider is the type of data. It is clear that all three variables are measured in ratio scale, i.e., they are all ratio data. Now the choice of a central tendency measure comes down to the shape of the histogram again. The histograms for "population" and "collection size" are both badly

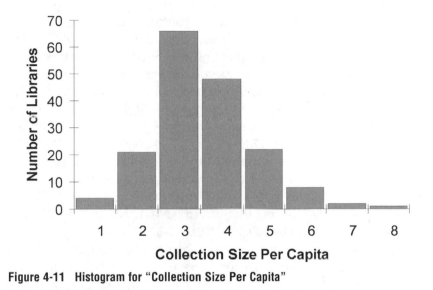

Figure 4-11   Histogram for "Collection Size Per Capita"

skewed so the median is the appropriate measure of central tendency. The histogram for "collection size per capita" is approximately
symmetrical although not perfect. Therefore, the mean will be an
appropriate measure of central tendency for this variable. The fact
that the mean of 3.05 is very close to the median of 2.84 for "collection size per capita" confirms that the distribution is not skewed
enough to call for the use of median. In contrast, for the two badly
skewed distributions of "population" and "collection size," there is a
huge discrepancy between the mean and the median, with the mean
being more than twice the median in both cases (see Figure 4-8).

To measure the variability of ratio data, we will use either standard
deviation or interquartile range (IQR). For a symmetrical distribution
like "collection size per capita," standard deviation is a better measure. For the two badly skewed distributions of "population" and "collection size," interquartile range is the preferred measure.
Unfortunately, Excel does not calculate IQR for us directly. However,
it is not difficult to get around with this problem by using Excel's "kth
largest" and "kth smallest" options, which are included in the popup
screen after you select the menu option "descriptive statistics." Here
you specify the number k for the "kth largest" and/or the "kth smallest" and Excel will tell you the value of these kth data points. For
example, if you specify k to be 26 for both the "kth largest" and the
"kth smallest," then Excel will display the values of the 26th largest

and the 26th smallest data points. If you happen to have 100 data points, then the difference between these two values will be the interquartile range (see definition of IQR in Section 4.2.2 of this chapter). If the number of data points you have is not this neat figure of 100, you can calculate the appropriate k value to obtain IQR. For the example data I am working with, there are 172 data points (the row labeled "Count" in Figure 4-8 shows the total number of data points). Because one quarter of 172 is 43 (i.e., 172/4=43), the difference between the 44th largest and the 44th smallest data points is IQR. So I specified k to be 44 and Excel included the values of these data points in the output (see the last two rows of Figure 4-8). A quick calculation shows IQR for "population" to be 41,107 (50,978-9,871) and for "collection size" to be 100,899 (132,924-32,025).

Now that we have decided what measures of descriptive statistics to use and what are the values for these measures, let us put them all together to see what conclusions we can reach about the libraries using these data; i.e., what the data tell us about these libraries. The skewed histogram of "population" tells us that these libraries served various sizes of populations with many libraries serving small populations (the left side of the histogram) and very few libraries serving large populations (the right side of the histogram). This reflects the pattern of population distribution in Ontario: There are many small cities and towns but very few medium to large urban centers. Indeed, the large interquartile range of 41,107 indicates great variability in the size of the populations served by the libraries. A typical library, however, served a population of 17,595 (the median). In other words, 50 percent of the libraries served a population greater than 17,595 and 50 percent of the libraries served a population smaller than this size. The shape of the histogram of "collection size" is very similar to that of "population" which means that many libraries had small collections and very few libraries had large collections. A typical library's collection size was 55,908 (the median) but the collection size varied greatly among libraries as indicated by the interquartile range of 100,899.

The fact that the frequency distribution of "collection size" mirrors that of "population" suggests that the collection size of a library was related to the size of the population it served. This speculation can be confirmed by an examination of the third variable "collection size per capita." The histogram of this variable is nowhere as skewed as those for the first two variables. Most data points sit fairly close to the center of the distribution. Indeed, the small standard deviation of 1.17 indicates a small variability among libraries in "collection size per capita," meaning that these libraries were more or less the same in this regard. This finding is not surprising given that public libraries are funded by tax dollars. The collection size is usually proportional to the size of the funding, which in turn is proportional to the tax base. A library serving a larger population will have a larger collection and vice versa. Therefore, on a per capita basis all the libraries had a similar size of collection, which works out an average of 3.05 (the mean) items per person.

For a further explanation of how central tendency and variability measures can be used together to make sense of data, let us look at another example. Consider the annual temperatures in two different places, Hawaii and New York. Even without the actual temperature data, we can imagine that Hawaii will have a higher mean (warmer on average) and lower standard deviation (temperatures do not vary much over the year). New York will have a lower mean (colder on average) and higher standard deviation (temperatures vary more over the year).

Yet another example of looking at mean and standard deviation together to obtain a complete picture is in choosing a mutual fund. If you only look at the mean of the fund's rates of return over the years without considering the volatility (the standard deviation of the rates of return), you may make a wrong decision. A fund that has a high mean rate of return may also have a high volatility (meaning that the rate fluctuates widely from year to year), which will make it a riskier investment. You need to consider both the rate of return (mean) and the volatility (standard deviation) in order to make a correct decision about whether to buy the fund.

CHAPTER 5

What Is Statistically Significant?—Basic Concepts of Inferential Statistics

I am certain that almost everyone in our society, regardless of whether or not they have anything to do with research, has heard the terms "statistically significant" or "not statistically significant." These terms appear in television news, newspapers, and magazines on topics ranging from politics to public health issues. Many people have difficulty understanding these terms and wonder what they really mean. The short answer is that they are important terms in inferential statistics. The detailed answer to the question will bring out many other terms. This chapter will explain all these terms and in so doing lead to the answer to the question of what is meant by "statistically significant." It is essentially an introduction to the basic concepts of inferential statistics. Reading this chapter will prepare you for the discussions of statistical tests in the rest of the book. So let us start with the question "what is inferential statistics?"

5.1 Descriptive Statistics vs. Inferential Statistics

There are two types of statistics: descriptive statistics and inferential statistics. The topics we have discussed so far, including graphical presentation of data and measures of central tendency and variability, are descriptive statistics. In descriptive statistics, we only summarize and describe the data without making any inference. For example, in a survey of 200 randomly selected university students, we asked respondents to report the average number of hours per week they spent on the Internet. If we describe the data by a histogram and report central tendency and variability of the data, we are using descriptive statistics. Most likely, however, we will not want to stop here. The purpose of the survey is probably to study the whole student body, not just these 200 particular students. Based on these 200 data points, we will try to estimate the number of hours per week all the university students, not just these 200, spent on the Internet. This extra step of making an estimate about the larger population based on a sample involves making an inference. The statistics we will use to make this calculated estimate or educated guess is called inferential statistics. In short, **descriptive statistics summarizes and characterizes the data set while inferential statistics uses the data set as a basis for making estimates or inferences.**

5.2 Population vs. Sample

In the above example, we try to estimate the hours spent on the Internet by the student population based on data collected from a sample of them. The terms "population" and "sample" have specific meanings in statistics. In the example, the term "population" refers to a group of people, which happens to be the same as the way we use the term in daily language. However, the statistical term "population" has a much broader meaning. Other than people, it can also refer to things or events. **A population, or universe, is defined as an entire group of persons, things, or events having at least one trait in common** (Sprinthall, 1997, 132). Thus, all the books in a library constitute a population because they have the common trait of belonging to the library. By the same token, all the reference transactions in a library are a population of events. **A sample is a subset of a population.** Fifty books from the library is a sample of the library book population and 30 reference transactions processed in a day is a sample of the reference transaction population for the year.

5.3 Parameter vs. Statistic

The purpose of inferential statistics is to make estimates about the population based on a sample. For instance, we can estimate the average number of hours per week students in a particular university spent on the Internet based on a survey of a sample of these university students. Here, the average number of hours per week for the sample students is known because we can calculate it easily from the data we collected, but the average number of hours for the entire student body is unknown and we are trying to estimate it. The former, the known, is called a statistic while the latter, the unknown, is called a parameter. **A statistic is any measure obtained by having measured a sample. A parameter is any measure obtained by having measured an entire population** (Sprinthall, 1997, 133). Notice that the statistical meaning of "parameter" is different from its meaning in daily language. If you have difficulty recalling whether parameter is associated with population or sample, just remember that "parameter" and "population" go together and that both start with "p." Similarly, remember that "statistic" and "sample" both begin with "s."

In inferential statistics, we estimate the parameter based on the statistic. This is called **parameter estimating**. The best examples of parameter estimating are pre-election polls or any of the other public opinion polls frequently encountered in the news. The advantage of inferential statistics in this situation is clear: It would be extremely expensive, if not impossible, to measure the entire population, so we take a sample of the population. We then estimate the parameter, the entire population's voting intention or opinion, based on the statistic, the voting intention or opinion of people in the sample. It is much more economical and efficient (the result is available much sooner) to measure the sample rather than the population. Of course, we will sacrifice some accuracy when we estimate rather than actually measure the population. Our estimate will not be 100 percent accurate nor with 100 percent certainty. Typically, pollsters will tell us that the result is accurate within x number of percentage points, usually 2 to 5 points, 19 times out of 20. How do they know the exact margin of error (x number of percentage points) and the chance that their prediction is correct (19 times out of 20)? The answer is that the prediction, or the statistical inference, is based on knowledge of probability and a very important distribution in statistics—the normal distribution.

5.4 Probability and Frequency Distribution

Probability theory, which originated in gambling, is the formal study of the laws of chance. Perhaps because of its roots in gambling, probability theory is best explained by tossing coins, rolling dice, or drawing cards. Probability can be defined as the number of times a specific event can occur out of the total possible number of events (Sprinthall, 1997, 108). According to this definition, the probability for the head to show up in a single toss of a coin is ½. (There is one head on the coin so the head can occur once. The coin has two sides so that there are two possible events.) Similarly, the probability of a "2" appearing when rolling a six-side die is 1 out of 6, or 0.17. When randomly drawing a card from a deck of 54, the probability of drawing a "10" regardless of the suit is 0.074 (4 out of 54). Anybody can do this kind of probability calculation without much difficulty. Why, then, does probability theory have a reputation for being very difficult and abstract among many people who have dealt with it as part of a statistics course? Because what we have just discussed is the simplest part of the probability theory. The advanced topics, including conditional probability, union and intersection of probability, and Bayes' theorem, are fairly complicated. They are useful in statistical formula deductions. For the practical use of statistics in research and decision-making, however, they are unnecessary. So, I will skip these topics and focus on the more important and easy-to-understand issue of probability and frequency distribution that is discussed below.

Suppose we have surveyed 100 students in a Canadian university on the number of hours per week they spent on the Internet (including using e-mail, browsing Web sites, etc.) and the data we collected are as shown in Figure 5-1. After inputting these data into Excel, we generated the histogram displayed in Figure 5-2.[1] Now imagine that I recorded each individual data point on a piece of paper, folded the paper and then put all 100 pieces of folded paper into a fish bowl. If I ask you to randomly pick a piece of paper from the bowl and report the data on it to me, what is the probability for the data you pick to be between 6 and 8? A close look at the data in Figure 5-1 will tell you that the answer is 0.34 because 34 out of 100 data points fall between 6 and 8. Similarly, the probability for the data to be between 8 and 10 is 0.13. Before you pick out the paper, if I ask you to bet on whether the data selected will be between 6 and 8 or between 8 and 10, you will bet on the former because the probability is higher there. If you then look at the histogram in Figure 5-2 you will see that the bars between 6 and 8 are taller than the bars between 8 and 10. What we have established through this exercise is that a histogram shows the probability and that the higher the bar in the histogram, the larger the area of the bar and the greater the probability for a data point to fall within the range of the bar.

For any histogram, you can connect the mid-point of the top of each bar to obtain a continuous curve. Figure 5-3 is the result of

1.0	1.5	2.0	2.5	2.5	2.6	3.0	3.1	3.1	3.2
3.5	3.5	3.5	3.6	3.7	3.9	4.1	4.1	4.2	4.3
4.5	4.5	4.5	4.5	4.5	5.0	5.0	5.0	5.0	5.0
5.0	5.1	5.2	5.2	5.2	5.5	5.5	5.5	5.5	5.5
5.5	5.5	5.5	5.7	5.7	5.8	5.8	5.9	5.9	5.9
6.2	6.2	6.3	6.3	6.4	6.5	6.5	6.5	6.5	6.5
6.5	6.5	6.5	6.5	6.6	6.6	6.7	6.8	6.9	7.1
7.1	7.2	7.2	7.3	7.3	7.5	7.5	7.5	7.5	7.5
7.8	7.8	7.9	7.9	8.1	8.2	8.3	8.4	8.5	8.5
8.5	8.6	8.6	9.2	9.5	9.5	9.5	10.5	11.0	12.0

Figure 5-1 Number of Hours per Week Spent on the Internet

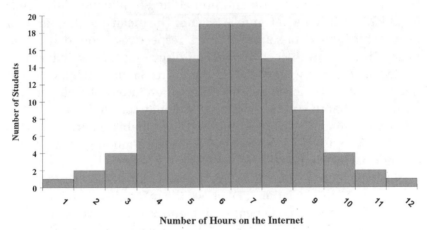

Figure 5-2 Histogram of Data in Figure 5-1

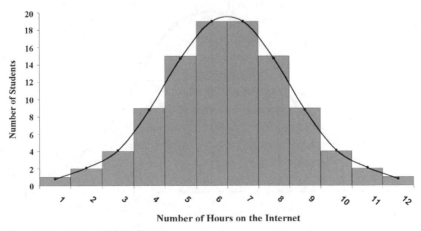

Figure 5-3 A Normal Distribution

applying this curve to the histogram in Figure 5-2. This curve gives us a better idea of the appearance of the distribution. The curve in Figure 5-3 resembles the bell-shaped symmetrical distribution called the normal distribution.

5.5 Normal Distribution

The normal distribution is the most important frequency distribution in statistics. It has some special characteristics, the most important and useful of which is that there is a constant relationship between standard deviation and probability. To illustrate this point, let us look at the data in Figure 5-1 again. The mean and the standard deviation of this data set are 6 and 2 respectively (rounded to the nearest integer for the convenience of discussion). As we have concluded in the discussion above, there are 34 data points valued between 6 and 8. Translating this observation into probability terms, we can say that the probability for a randomly selected data point to fall between 6 and 8 is 0.34. Similarly, the probability between 8 and 10 is 0.135. Figure 5-4 is a graphical demonstration of probability for this normal distribution.[2]

Since the mean is 6 and the standard deviation is 2, we can say that 8 is one standard deviation (SD) above the mean (because 6 + 2 = 8). Thus "1SD" is displayed beneath 8 in Figure 5-4. Similarly, 4 is 1 standard deviation below the mean so "-1SD" is displayed beneath 4 (the "-" sign means below the mean). The same interpretation applies to

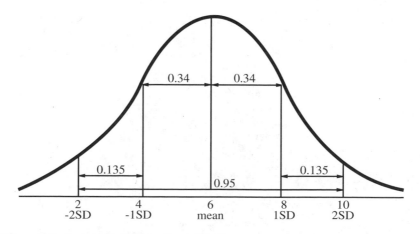

Figure 5-4   Probability Under a Normal Curve

"-2SD" and "2SD" in the Figure. Figure 5-4 tells us that the probability for a data point to fall between the mean and one standard deviation is 0.34. Since the graph is symmetrical, we can say that **the probability for a randomly selected data point to fall within one standard deviation from the mean is 0.68** (calculated by adding together 0.34 below the mean and 0.34 above the mean). Similarly, **the probability for a data point to fall within two standard deviations from the mean is 0.95.** This constant relationship between standard deviation and probability holds for any normal distribution regardless of what variables we are dealing with (be it people's height or weight or pulse rate). As long as the frequency distribution is normal, we know that 68 percent of data points are located within one standard deviation from the mean and 95 percent of data points lie within two standard deviations from the mean.

5.6 The Z Score

In Figure 5-4, we have two different measuring units displayed at the base line of the distribution. The first one is in the number of hours (2, 4, 6, etc.), the original unit we used to measure the time spent on the Internet. The other one is the number of standard deviations from the mean (-1SD, 1SD, 2SD, etc.). This new measuring unit is called the Z score. The way we converted the data from the original unit to the Z score is:

$$Z = \frac{x - \bar{x}}{SD}$$

where $\bar{x}$ is the mean, SD stands for standard deviation, and x is the original value for which we are calculating the Z score. A positive Z score means that the data point lies above the mean and a negative one below the mean. It is very easy to calculate Z scores for any data set once we know the mean and the standard deviation. For instance, to find the Z score for x = 2 in the example data set, just plug x = 2, $\bar{x}$ = 6, SD = 2 into the formula, and we get -2. This means that 2 is 2 standard deviations below the mean. This is why "-2SD" is displayed beneath 2 in Figure 5-4. I have heard people say, "Z score is the beginning of confusion in statistics." I hope that you will not reach this conclusion here. If you do not like the term "Z score," just think of it as the number of standard deviations from the mean. A Z score of 2 means 2 standard deviations above the mean while a Z score of -1.5 means 1.5 standard deviations below the mean.

Why do we want to convert the original data into this strange sounding Z score? We do this conversion because the Z score enables us to compare data from two different distributions or even data from two different variables directly. To explain this point, let us suppose that the data in Figure 5-1 were collected in a Canadian university. Now, let us further suppose that a similar survey has been conducted in a university in China and the data show a normal distribution with a mean of 4 and a standard deviation of 1. On average, the Chinese students spent less time on the Internet than their Canadian counterparts (a mean of 4 as oppose to a mean of 6 for the Canadian students).

If John, a Canadian student, spent 5 hours per week on the Internet and Wong, a Chinese student, spent 4.5 hours a week, who spent more time on the Internet relative to their peers? You cannot compare the data of the two students directly and say that John spent more. In fact, John's number is below the average for the Canadian students while Wong's is above the average for the Chinese students. If we calculate the Z scores for the two students, we can then compare them directly. Using the formula on the previous page, we calculate that John's Z score is -0.5 while Wong's is 0.5 as shown in Table 5-1. Since 0.5 is greater than -0.5, we can conclude that Wong spent relatively more time on the Internet than John did. This example illustrates that the Z score is a relative rank or relative standing score. Because of this, we can compare scores from two different distributions directly.

Table 5-1   Comparison of Hours on the Internet Between Two Students

	John (Canadian student $\bar{x}=6$, SD=2)	**Wong** (Chinese student $\bar{x}=4$, SD=1)
Hours	x=5	x=4.5
Z score	$Z=(x-\bar{x})/SD = (5-6)/2 = -0.5$	$Z=(x-\bar{x})/SD = (4.5-4)/1 = 0.5$

In fact, we can even use Z scores to compare data from two different variables directly. Suppose that in the Canadian survey, you also asked the respondents to report the number of hours per week they spent in the university library. The data collected show a normal distribution with a mean of 3 and a standard deviation of 1. John reported spending 4 hours per week in the library and 5 hours per week on the Internet. There are two variables here, "the number of hours spent in the library" and "the number of hours spent on the Internet." We cannot compare data from these two different variables directly just as we cannot compare somebody's weight figure with his/her height figure. However, we can compare Z scores from two different variables directly. Because John's Z score for hours in the library is 1 and his Z score for hours on the Internet is -0.5, we can conclude that relative to his peers John spent more time in the library (above average) and less time on the Internet (below average). This statement does not contradict the fact that he spent one more hour per week on the Internet than in the library.

5.7 Standard Normal Distribution

When comparing John and Wong's time on the Internet, we have concluded that Wong spent relatively more time on the Internet than John did because Wong's Z score is 0.5 while John's is -0.5. Wong is above average among Chinese students and John is below average among Canadian students. To further know the relative standing of John and Wong among their peers, we may ask, "exactly what percent of Chinese students are below Wong" and "exactly what percent of Canadian students are above John." Figure 5-4 tells us the probability of being above or below 1 or 2 standard deviations (i.e., for Z scores of 1 or 2) but it does not show the probability for a Z score of 0.5.

To know the exact probability associated with any Z score, we can use the standard normal distribution table shown in Appendix 1.[3] In fact, the probability figures in Figure 5-4 come from this table. For instance, the table shows that the probability between the mean and a Z score of 1.00 (1 standard deviation) is 0.3413. When rounded to two decimal points, this is the same as the probability shown in Figure 5-4. To know what percent of Chinese students Wong is above, just check the probability for Z of 0.5, which the Table shows as 0.1915. So Wong is above 69.15 percent of Chinese students (calculated as 50 percent of students below the mean plus 19.15 percent between the mean and 0.5 standard deviation. Please see Figure 5-5 for a clearer image). Similarly, John, whose Z score is -0.5, is below 69.15 percent of Canadian students. Or to state it differently, John is above 30.85 percent of Canadian students (see Figure 5-5 again).

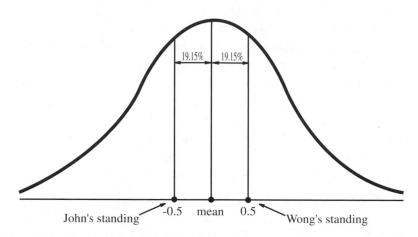

Figure 5-5   Wong and John's Relative Standing Among Their Peers

For any normal distribution, once the original scores are converted into Z scores, the standard normal distribution table can be used to find out the relative standing or the probability associated with the scores. Here we see the beauty of a normal distribution: as long as you know the mean and the standard deviation of the distribution, you can estimate approximately what proportion of the data points will be in a particular range. For instance, we know that IQ scores follow a normal distribution. Suppose that you took an IQ test that has a mean of 100 and a standard deviation of 10 and you scored 115. Converting your raw IQ score (115) into the Z score, we get 1.5. This means that you are 1.5 standard deviations above the mean. The standard normal distribution table shows that the probability between the mean and the Z score of 1.5 is 0.4332 (see Appendix 1). Hence, we can conclude that you are above 93.32 percent of the people in the IQ score (50 percent people below the mean plus 43.32 percent between the mean and 1.5 standard deviation).

5.8 Confidence Interval

The preceding discussions on probability, Z score, and the normal distribution have paved our way to answer the question raised earlier in the chapter: "How do pollsters know the exact margin of error (x number of percentage points) and the chance that their prediction is correct (19 times out of 20)?"

Recall the logic of inferential statistics discussed earlier: We cannot afford to measure, or it is impossible to measure, the whole population, so we take a sample and estimate the population based on the sample. For example, before a national referendum where people will vote "yes" or "no" to a question, it is too expensive and, in all likelihood, impossible to survey every potential voter. Therefore, a polling firm will take a sample of voters and ask them how they are going to vote. If the sample is unbiased and truly represents the population, the proportion of "yes" voters (or "no" voters) in the sample will be fairly close to the proportion of "yes" voters (or "no" voters) in the population. It will not be exactly the same because we may happen to have a few more "yes" voters or a few more "no" voters in the sample, which is quite possible given the random nature of the sampling. The "yes" proportion or the "no" proportion in the sample will then be larger than that in the population. However, common sense tells us that the sample proportion should not depart too far from the population proportion. In other words, the chance for a large discrepancy to happen is very slim.

If you take a sample again and again, you will get many sample proportions and they will all be slightly different from each other. However, most of them will be fairly close to the population proportion. If you plot these sample proportions in a frequency distribution, they will show a normal distribution. The center of this distribution will be the population proportion—the proportion that the pollsters are actually trying to estimate. This is essentially what the central limit theorem, a very important statistical theorem, tells us. I will skip the technical discussion of the theorem here but will give a graphical explanation as shown in Figure 5-6.

Figure 5-6 shows that the probability for a sample proportion to deviate very far away from the population proportion is very small (the tail part of the distribution) while a small departure is most likely (the middle part of the distribution). From the discussion we had earlier on probability and normal distribution, we know that the probability for a data point in a normal distribution to fall within two standard deviations from the mean is 0.95. Translating this statement into the normal distribution in Figure 5-6, we can say that the probability for a single sample proportion to fall within two standard deviations from the population proportion (located in the center of the distribution in Figure 5-6) is 0.95. In other words, if the pollsters give a margin of error of two standard deviations, then they have a 95 percent chance of being correct, which is the same as being correct "19 times out of 20." For example, if the proportion of "yes" voters in the sample is 45 percent and the standard deviation of the distribution in Figure 5-6 is 1.5, then the margin of error will be 3 (two standard deviations).[4] So the pollsters can predict a 45 percent "yes" vote given a margin of error of 3 percent and they can claim a 95 percent chance of being correct in this prediction. This can also be stated as the familiar "we predict a 45 percent yes vote with a margin of error of plus or minus 3 percentage points. The prediction is accurate 19 times out of 20."

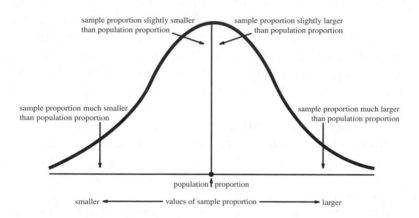

Figure 5-6   Normal Distribution of Sample Proportions

When pollsters predict a 45 percent yes vote given a margin of error of 3 percent, they are saying that the yes vote in the population can be anywhere between 42 percent to 48 percent and they are 95 percent sure of this prediction. In statistics, this range of 42 to 48 is called the **confidence interval** and the 95 percent chance or 0.95 probability is called the **confidence level**. The commonly used confidence level is 0.95 (this is why pollsters always use the "19 times out of 20" level). You can make predictions at other confidence levels, but the confidence interval will change accordingly. The relationship between confidence interval and confidence level is that when the confidence level increases, the confidence interval will increase too. We do not need to prove this statistically. Just imagine that if I ask you to predict tomorrow's daytime high temperature and I want you to be

50 percent sure of your prediction (confidence level of 0.5), you can give me a fairly narrow range, say between 68°F to 71°F. But if I require you to be 95 percent sure (confidence level increases to 0.95) then you will give me a wider range, say 65°F to 74°F, just to be safe (confidence interval increases, too).

So far we have discussed how to estimate population proportion based on sample proportion. The same logic and process applies to estimating population mean based on sample mean, e.g., estimating the average height of a group of people based on the height of a sample of these people. The mathematical formulae involved in these two estimation processes are different but the results are interpreted in the same way. We will omit the math formula part of the confidence interval because it involves concepts that many people find confusing, such as standard error, mean of the distribution of means, etc. Besides, a discussion of these technical details will not help much in interpreting the results anyway. We will just use an example to show how to use computer software to calculate the confidence interval. We will then discuss what the result tells us.

Suppose we want to know the average number of hours per week graduate students in a university spent in the university library. We took a random sample of 100 of these students and asked them to report the hours they spent in the library in the past week. We can then estimate the average hours of all the graduate students based on this sample data. To analyze the data using SPSS, we input the 100 data points into the software as a variable (a column), click the menu items "Analyze," "Descriptive Statistics," and "Explore," and then specify the variable. We will get the output as shown in Figure 5-7.

			Statistic	Std. Error
HOURS	Mean		5.915	0.210
	95% Confidence	Lower Bound	5.500	
	Interval for Mean	Upper Bound	6.331	
	5% Trimmed Mean		5.928	
	Median		5.982	
	Variance		4.392	
	Std. Deviation		2.096	
	Minimum		1.0	
	Maximum		10.5	
	Range		9.5	
	Interquartile Range		3.000	
	Skewness		0.007	0.241
	Kurtosis		-0.536	0.478

Figure 5-7 Confidence Interval Estimated by SPSS (confidence level 0.95)

The sample mean is calculated at 5.9, which is the average number of hours per week these 100 students spent in the library. We want to estimate the average number of hours per week all the graduate students spent in the library, i.e., the population mean. The confidence interval gives us this estimate. Based on the sample data, SPSS calculated the confidence interval to be between 5.5 ("Lower Bound" in Figure 5-7) and 6.3 ("Upper Bound" in Figure 5-7). This means that there is a 95 percent chance that the population mean is somewhere between 5.5 and 6.3. In other words, we do not know the exact average hours but we can be 95 percent certain that it is somewhere between 5.5 and 6.3 hours. Translating this result into pollsters' language, we can say that the average number of hours per week that graduate students spent in the library is 5.9, the margin of error of this estimate is 0.4 hours (calculated as (6.3-5.5)/2). This estimate is accurate 19 times out of 20.

Most statistical software sets the confidence level at 0.95 by default, but you can change this default level easily and calculate the confidence interval at whatever level you want. I changed the confidence level into 0.99 and let SPSS calculate the confidence interval again. The output is shown in Figure 5-8. All the statistical results in Figure 5-8 are the same as those in Figure 5-7 other than the confidence interval values that are now 5.4 and 6.5. The confidence interval is wider for the 0.99 level than for the 0.95 level, which proves the point made earlier—the confidence interval increases as the confidence level increases.

			Statistic	Std. Error
HOURS	Mean		5.915	0.210
	99% Confidence	Lower Bound	5.365	
	Interval for Mean	Upper Bound	6.466	
	5% Trimmed Mean		5.928	
	Median		5.982	
	Variance		4.392	
	Std. Deviation		2.096	
	Minimum		1.0	
	Maximum		10.5	
	Range		9.5	
	Interquartile Range		3.000	
	Skewness		0.007	0.241
	Kurtosis		-0.536	0.478

Figure 5-8   Confidence Interval Estimated by SPSS (confidence level 0.99)

5.9 Hypothesis Testing—Statistically Significant or Not

The above calculation of the 95 percent confidence interval tells us that the average number of hours per week graduate students spent in the library is somewhere between 5.5 and 6.3 and we can be 95 percent sure with this estimate. What would you say if somebody claims that the average hours are eight per week? If you have to make a decision to reject or accept this claim or hypothesis, what would you do? I bet you will reject it because probability theory supports you; you have at least a 95 percent chance of being correct in this decision. On the other hand, if someone hypothesizes that the average hours spent in the library is six, you will not reject this hypothesis because it is within the interval (5.5 to 6.3) that we are confident about. This decision of rejecting or not rejecting a hypothesis is called hypothesis testing, and the logic of it is fairly straightforward, as we have just discussed. It is obvious that confidence interval and hypothesis testing are closely related. In fact, they can be viewed as two sides of the same coin.

The process of hypothesis testing can be summarized as follows. We assume that the hypothesis is true. We then collect data to test the hypothesis. Based on the data we can calculate the confidence interval and the probability that the hypothesis is true. If the probability that the hypothesis is true is smaller than a pre-set level, usually 0.05, we will reject the hypothesis; otherwise we will not reject it. I will use an example to illustrate how a hypothesis testing is carried out.

Suppose a university library wants to test the effect of students' knowledge of the library on the amount of time they will spend in the library. The library staff offered workshops and tutorials on how to make better use of the library resources to students in a particular graduate program, for instance, the journalism program. Students generally became more knowledgeable about the library as a result of this library education. Does this library education program affect the amount of time students spend in the library? A random sample of 50 journalism students was surveyed on the number of hours per week they now spend in the library. Suppose we know from a previous survey (before the library education) that the average number of hours these students spent in the library was six per week. The hypothesis to be tested is that the average hours spent in the library is not 6 per week anymore. The statistical procedure to test the hypothesis is as follows.

STEP 1: We formulate two competing hypotheses, the null hypothesis and the alternative hypothesis. The null hypothesis, symbolized as H_0, is that the average hours remained unchanged, i.e., that the students spent an average of six hours per week in the library. The alternative hypothesis, symbolized as H_a is that the average number of hours changed, i.e., it is now different from six. It must be emphasized that the null hypothesis always assumes no change or no difference even if you strongly believe that there is a change and intend to prove this. The logic of statistical tests requires us to follow this rule. If this requirement is not met, the test result and thus the conclusion reached will be opposite to the truth. The procedure for a hypothesis test is parallel to that of a criminal trial. Even if you strongly believe that the accused is guilty, you have to start with the assumption of innocence.

STEP 2: We calculate the test statistic using the sample data collected. You may think that we should calculate the confidence interval because I said earlier that confidence interval and hypothesis testing are two sides of the same coin. You are correct in this thought because the formula for the test statistic and the formula for the confidence interval are mathematically equivalent. We will not get into the details of the formula for the test statistic because computer software can easily do the calculations for us. We just have to know that the data we collected will be summarized into a single figure called the test statistic and we will use it as the evidence to assess the null hypothesis.

STEP 3: Determine the probability that the null hypothesis is true (called p-value) based on the test statistic. Essentially, the p-value is the probability of obtaining a test statistic equal to the one we have if the null hypothesis were true. It follows that a smaller p-value is stronger evidence against the null hypothesis. In other words, the smaller the p-value, the less likely that the null hypothesis is true.

STEP 4: Compare the p-value to a pre-set significance level α, usually 0.05. If the p-value is equal to or less than α, we will reject the null hypothesis and accept the alternative hypothesis. We can thus conclude that the difference is statistically significant. If the p-value is greater than the significance level α, we fail to reject the null hypothesis; i.e., we have insufficient evidence to say that the null hypothesis is wrong.

These four steps are the same for all statistical tests including the tests that will be discussed in later chapters. For the particular example we are discussing, we have stated the hypothesis, which is step 1. The next step is to calculate the test statistic, in this case the t score. The test is thus called the t test. Since we only have one sample, the 50 journalism students, as opposed to two samples, which we will discuss in later chapters, we should do a one-sample t test. After inputting the 50 hypothetical data points into SPSS as a variable (a column), I went through menu options of "Analyze," "Compare Means," and "One-Sample T Test." I then specified the test value to be six (the average of six hours per week stated in the null hypothesis). The SPSS output is as shown in Figure 5-9.

One-Sample Statistics

	N	Mean	Std. Deviation	Std. Error Mean
HOURS	50	6.7600	1.9749	.2793

One-Sample Test

	Test Value = 6					
				Mean Difference	95% Confidence Interval of the Difference	
	t	df	Sig. (2-tailed)		Lower	Upper
HOURS	2.721	49	.009	.7600	.1987	1.3213

Figure 5-9 SPSS Output for One Sample T Test (the case of statistically significant)

The t score, which is the test statistic, is calculated at 2.721. Based on this t score, SPSS calculated the p-value to be 0.009 (the value in the last row of the fourth column, the second table of Figure 5-9). This p-value tells us that the probability for the null hypothesis to be true is only 0.009, i.e., a nine per thousand chance. The last step is to compare this p-value against the pre-set significance level of 0.05 (this is the most commonly used significance level). Since p-value is less than 0.05, we can reject the null hypothesis, which assumed that the average hours remained the same.

The SPSS output also gives us some extra information. The average number of hours for the sample students is 6.76 (shown as "Mean" in the first table of Figure 5-9), which is 0.76 hours higher than the hypothesized value of six. This increase of 0.76 hour is displayed under "Mean Difference" in the second table. Although the average increase among the sample students is 0.76 hour, we do not know the exact increase in the population (all the journalism students).

However, we can be 95 percent sure that it will be somewhere between 0.2 to 1.3 hours (see values under "95% Confidence Interval of the Difference" in the second table, rounded to one decimal point). Based on this data analysis result, we can conclude that the library education program does have an effect on the amount of time students spend in the library. There is an average increase of 0.76 hour and this increase is statistically significant.

If the SPSS output is as shown in Figure 5-10, our conclusion will be very different from what we have just discussed. This time the T score is 0.259, the p-value of which is 0.797. Because the p-value is greater than the significance level of 0.05, we fail to reject the null hypothesis. In other words, we have insufficient evidence to prove that the library education had an effect on the hours students spend in the library. Notice that the mean is calculated at 6.084, an increase of 0.084 hour compared to the average of six hours stated in the null hypothesis. This slight increase of the mean in the sample can be viewed as a random result, i.e., the sample happened to include a few students who spent more hours in the library. The confidence interval further confirms the conclusion from the hypothesis testing. We can be 95 percent sure that the difference between the population mean and the hypothesized mean of six is anywhere between -0.569 and 0.737. This confidence interval includes zero, which means that the difference could be zero so that the average hours remained at six. We can say that the effect of the library education program on time spent in the library is not statistically significant.

One-Sample Statistics

	N	Mean	Std. Deviation	Std. Error Mean
HOURS	50	6.0840	2.2977	.3249

One-Sample Test

	Test Value = 6					
					95% Confidence Interval of the Difference	
	t	df	Sig. (2-tailed)	Mean Difference	Lower	Upper
HOURS	.259	49	.797	8.400E-02	-.5690	.7370

Figure 5-10 SPSS Output for One Sample T Test (the case of not statistically significant)

5.10 Errors of Statistical Testing—Type I and Type II Errors

It is clear from the logic of hypothesis testing that statistical decisions on whether or not we reject the null hypothesis are based on probability. Specifically, if the probability for the null hypothesis to be true (the p-value) is smaller than the pre-set level, usually 0.05, we reject the null hypothesis. On the other hand, if the probability or the p-value is greater than 0.05, we will not reject the null hypothesis. These statistical decisions are mostly likely to be correct, having at least a 95 percent chance of being correct. However, we are not 100 percent certain of our decisions. There is always a chance, no matter how slim, that our decision will be wrong, i.e., we will have a statistical error. It should be noted that having a statistical error does not mean that we made a mistake in data collection or data analysis. Rather, statistical errors are rooted in the very nature of statistical decisions, decisions that are based on probability. There are two types of statistical errors: type I error, also called the alpha error, and type II error, also called beta error. I will keep using the example that we have been working with in the previous section to explain these two types of errors.

The statistical decision we made based on the result in Figure 5-9 was to reject the null hypothesis because the p-value, the probability that the null hypothesis is correct, is only 0.009. In other words, if the population mean is six as assumed by the null hypothesis, there is only a 9 per thousand chance that we will get the t score of 2.721 that is shown in Figure 5-9. Thus we had a 0.991 probability or a 99.1 percent chance of being correct when we rejected the null hypothesis. However, there was still a 0.9 percent chance that the null hypothesis is correct but we wrongly rejected it. If this is what happened, then a type I error has occurred. **Type I error occurs when the null hypothesis is correct and we reject it.** By definition, type I error can occur only when we reject the null hypothesis. If the null hypothesis is not rejected, then type I error is irrelevant but there is a chance of having another type of error, the type II error, which is discussed below.

We decided not to reject the null hypothesis based on the result in Figure 5-10 because the probability for the null hypothesis to be true was calculated at 0.797. In other words, it is fairly likely (a 79.7 percent chance) that the population mean is 6 as stated in the null hypothesis. Therefore we cannot reject the null hypothesis. However, the chance for the null hypothesis to be true is not 100 percent. It is possible that the null hypothesis is wrong and the population mean is higher than six, say 6.3. However, the sample happened to include a few more data points on the low end (possible for a random sample) so we ended up with a sample mean of 6.08 as shown in Figure 5-10. If this is the case, then a type II error has occurred. **Type II error occurs when the null hypothesis is wrong but we fail to reject it.** Clearly, type II error can only occur if we do not reject the null hypothesis.

Table 5-2 summarizes all the possible scenarios associated with a statistical decision. The distinction between type I and type II errors is clearer from the table. Table 5-2 shows that no matter what statistical decisions we make about the null hypothesis, there is always a chance of error. This is understandable because we never know the absolute truth of the population—if we knew, there would be no need to do a statistical test. All we are doing in inferential statistics is to estimate the population based on a sample by employing knowledge of probability theory. By definition, nothing is absolutely certain in estimating and inference based on probability is inescapably attended by the chance of errors. The purpose of discussing statistical errors is to demonstrate that a statistical conclusion is an educated guess rather than the absolute truth. If your statistical analysis will be the basis for somebody's major decision, it is a good idea to mention the disclaimer—the possible statistical error associated with your conclusion.

Table 5-2   Statistical Decisions and Errors

	Null hypothesis is correct	Null hypothesis is wrong
Null hypothesis rejected	Type I error	Correct decision
Null hypothesis not rejected	Correct decision	Type II error

Endnotes

1. The data here are artificially made up for the convenience of discussion. In a real survey, respondents are more likely to report time by hour, half hour, or quarter hour rather than a fraction of hour such as 0.8. In real data collection, it is not likely that you would get a perfectly symmetrical distribution like the one in Figure 5-2.

2. Note that the probability of 0.14 is changed into 0.135 for a more accurate statement of probability for normal distributions.

3. There is a mathematical formula to calculate the exact probability under a normal curve for different Z scores. However, this formula involves calculus, which is beyond the scope of this book. For practical use of the normal distribution, we can consult this table, which shows the results of that calculation, without worrying about how the table is calculated.

4. The standard deviation of Figure 5-6 is called standard error. There is a formula to calculate standard error but we will omit these technical details here.

CHAPTER 6

How to Collect Data— Sampling Methods

As discussed in the previous chapter, the purpose of inferential statistics is to make inferences about the population based on the sample. Using probability theory, we can state with a certain level of confidence, usually 95 percent, that our inference will be correct. Statistical calculations can also tell us the margin of error of our prediction. However, it must be emphasized that all these inferences and calculations are based on the assumption that the sample is sufficiently representative of the population. If this prerequisite is not met, the foundation of the inference falls apart and the stated confidence level and margin of error will be meaningless. No probability theory or mathematical formula can produce an accurate inference based on a biased or unrepresentative sample. We must always keep this principle in mind whenever we read statistical results, regardless of whether they are from research literature or from media reports. By the same token, we must make every effort to ensure that the samples we use in our own research are unbiased. What sampling methods are available to ensure that the sample represents the population? This is what we will discuss in this chapter.

6.1 Simple Random Sample

The simple random sample is one of the most commonly used sampling methods. It requires that each member of the population has an equal and independent chance of being selected. Because each member has the same chance of being chosen, it is unbiased and thus considered to be an "ideal" sampling method. To give each member of the population the same chance, every member must first be identified. This requires a list of the entire population called the sampling frame.

Once the sampling frame is available, the process of selecting the members from it is quite simple. You can code the members in the list from 1 to N, the total number of members. Then, you select the members to be included in the sample according to a random number list. To illustrate, if the random number list is 56, 78, 90…, then members 56, 78, 90, etc., should be selected. The question is where you get the random number list. The classical method is to use a table of random numbers such as the one shown in Appendix 2. This is still the method that many current textbooks recommend. You start with the first number in the table and then go either horizontally or vertically to use the next number. Suppose that there are 7,000 members in your sampling frame and you want to take a random sample of 100 members. If you decide to go vertically in the random number table, then you will select member 3,894, 1,005, 5,970, 8,981, etc. Since your population size is 7,000, member 8,981 does not exist in your sampling frame. You can simply ignore this number and move on to the next number that is in your sampling frame, in this case 130, until you get 100 members in your sample.

Nowadays, a much more convenient and efficient way of taking a random sample is to use a computer to generate the list of random numbers. Most statistical and spreadsheet software has this function. For example, Excel 2000 has a "Random Number Generation" menu item under "Data Analysis." You can easily specify the beginning and ending number of the sampling frame as well as the sample size required. One of the advantages of using software as opposed to a random number table is that you can use the software to sort the random numbers generated, thus avoiding the problem of constantly moving back and forth in the sampling frame to search for the corresponding case. Using a computer to take a random sample is even more convenient if the sampling frame is in the computer already. Imagine that you are doing a survey of the students in a university and the registrar's office is willing to provide the list of students in a computer file. You can then take a random sample directly from the list without having to go through the process of coding the sampling frame and generating the random numbers. Again, most statistical software can do this easily.

In many practical situations, a complete list of the population does not exist or it exists but is not accessible for various reasons. Even where a list is available, coding the list for the purpose of a random sample may be prohibitively costly or time-consuming. In these situations, there are alternative methods that are more efficient and cost-effective than a simple random sample. The systematic sample is one of them.

6.2   Systematic Sample

A systematic sample starts at a randomly chosen member of the population and then takes every nth member afterward. For instance, if you have 10,000 members in the population and want to take a sample of 50 of them, you would start at a randomly chosen member, say the 10th member, and sample every 200th member afterward (10,000/50 = 200). Thus member 10, 210, 410, etc., will be included in the sample. Systematic sample still guarantees that each member of the population has the same opportunity of being chosen so this sampling method is an unbiased and acceptable one. Indeed, the results from systematic samples tend to be slightly more accurate than results from simple random samples, but inconsequentially so. The orderly sampling process allows less opportunity for sampling error to occur (Hopkins and Glass, 1978, 187).

The chief advantage of systematic sampling over simple random sampling is its efficiency; i.e., it is less time-consuming. There is no need to code the members of the population nor is there a need for a random number list. The advantage of this improved efficiency is particularly obvious when the population size is so large that coding the entire population will be extremely time-consuming. Imagine that you want to take a sample of 200 books from a library that has 20,000 books (in fact, this is a very small library). Coding every book alone will take a lot of time. In contrast, taking every 100th book for a systematic sample is much easier. An even more efficient method without compromising the quality of the sample too much is to measure or estimate the total length of shelf space of the library and then take a book from every Xth feet of the shelf length.

The down side of the systematic sample is its sensitivity to the periodic nature of the population character being studied. If you want to determine the average number of visitors per day in an information center over a year, you can randomly select some days from a calendar and record the number of visitors in those days to estimate the yearly average. However, if you take a systematic sample of the days, say every 14th or 28th day, you will end up with the same days of the week in your sample. If Fridays are being selected and Friday is a low day in the information center, you will under estimate the average number of visitors. Similarly, your estimate will be inflated if you happen to choose a busy day in the week. Even if you choose a number that is not a multiple of seven (e.g., every ninth day), you may still not have a proper representation of all days of the week.

Many other things also have this kind of periodic nature; e.g., number of circulation transactions in a public or academic library. Apparently, a simple random sample is better than a systematic sample in this kind of situation. If there is a strong pattern of variation over different days in a week and you want to ensure that all of the different days are properly represented in the sample, a stratified sample, discussed below, is better than a simple random sample.

6.3 Stratified Sample

A stratified sample, short for stratified random sample, involves dividing the population into more homogeneous subgroups or strata from which simple random samples are then taken (Levin and Fox, 1997, 142). In the above example of selecting days to estimate the number of visitors per day to an information center, you can divide the population, all the days that the center opens, into strata of Monday, Tuesday, Wednesday, etc., and then randomly select an equal number of days from each stratum. This sample will give you a better estimate of the average number of visitors per day over the year than a simple random sample if the number of visitors varies greatly among different days of the week.

A stratified random sample can be proportional or disproportionate. The above example is a proportional stratified sample if the information center opens for the same number of Mondays, Tuesdays, etc., over the year. If the center will be closed on some Mondays for long weekend holidays, then a proportional stratified sample will require reducing the number of Mondays in the sample proportionally. For instance, if it opens 25 Mondays and 50 Tuesdays in a year, then you should select twice as many Tuesdays as Mondays for a proportional sample. For a disproportionate sample, you can select the same number of Mondays and Tuesdays regardless of how many more Tuesdays are open. As long as disproportionate substrata are analyzed comparatively, the disproportionate sampling methods need not alarm us (Walsh, 1990, 81). This means that if we are to compare the number of visitors Monday vs. Tuesday, then a disproportionate sample is fine. However, if we are to combine different weekdays together to estimate the average number of visitors per day in a year, then a proportional sample should be obtained.

When the population becomes more diverse in its characteristics, selecting a representative sample becomes more difficult. In these situations, a simple random sample does not always guarantee representativeness due to its randomness—the sample may happen to include more members with certain characteristics. A stratified sample is an attempt to ensure the representativeness of subgroups or strata. The trait with which the population is divided into strata should be selected carefully. If you are designing a stratified sample to study the use of a paid online information service by a university community, one of the meaningful ways of stratifying would be by type of users; e.g., faculty members, undergraduate students, and graduate students. Faculty members have more means, e.g., research grants, to pay for the service than students do. Stratifying people by their weight or height would be meaningless in this case.

There are other ways of selecting a sample that are not discussed in this book due to space limitations. Some are designed to ensure representativeness and others for cost-effectiveness. You can create a sampling method that is a variation of an existing method and that suits your particular situation and needs as long as you can justify that it is not biased.

6.4 Sampling Bias

Obtaining a truly unbiased sample is easier in physical sciences than in social sciences. Lab mice selected in a random sampling will all participate in the study; they do not have a choice. A sample of randomly selected university students, however, may not all be willing to participate. This kind of self-selection bias exists in most social science studies. We should make every effort to minimize this problem. Textbooks on research methods often have in-depth discussions of this issue. If the sampling method is proper and there is no systematic bias, the result can be accurate even if the participation rate is not 100 percent, as is evidenced by the accuracy of some well done modern pre-election polls.

However, many studies did not have a proper sampling method to start with, nor did the researchers make efforts to overcome possible bias. Magazines often "sample" people's opinions on a particular issue by including a questionnaire in the magazine. Two problems are obvious here. First, readers of a particular magazine are not a random sample of the general population in a society. When reading any research result or media report, we always need to be aware of what kind of population a sample is representing. Second, the sample obtained this way may not even represent the readers of this magazine. Often only people who feel strongly about the issue or who are highly motivated for whatever reason will return the questionnaire. Thus this method is improper even for the magazine's own readership survey. Even more biased are the opinions solicited through a telephone 900 number or a phone-in show. People who do not want to pay for the phone call or do not have time to call when the show is on are excluded from the sample.

There has been a series of surveys conducted on the Web that regularly collect data on demographic profiles of Web users and solicited user opinions on issues related to the Web. The surveys were advertised at various Web sites, list servers, and news groups. Thousands of people participated in the surveys by filling out a Web-based questionnaire. The questionnaire may have been well designed and the sample size is very large. The sampling method, however, renders the results unreliable. Not all Web users have an equal opportunity to participate. Infrequent or novice users have a lower chance of seeing the advertisements and probably have less inclination to go to the designated Web site and fill out the questionnaire. The sample does not represent the Web user population very well, let alone the general public in a society where many people have never used the Web. This biased sample will generate biased results. For example, some people analyzed the "income" data from the survey and concluded that there was no significant income difference between men and women. The fact is that only a small percent of survey participants were women and they were typically well educated and had well paid jobs, not a representative sample of the women in our society at all.

The sampling bias may not be as obvious in some cases. We have all seen those interviewers standing at a downtown street corner or in a shopping mall. They dress up professionally and approach every 5th or 10th person who walks by to conduct surveys. It looks like everybody passing them has an equal opportunity of being interviewed. However, not everybody in the community goes to downtown or the mall with the same frequency. Furthermore, some type of people may be systematically excluded depending on the time of day that the survey is conducted. A daytime survey excludes all the people who work during daytime.

Similar examples exist in information science. Libraries, public or academic, sometimes conduct surveys of people who walk into the library. Those who visit the library more frequently will have more opportunities to be included. If the purpose of the study is to find out users' satisfaction level with the library's service and how the service can be improved, the results will definitely be biased because you will miss those who are dissatisfied with the service and have stopped going to the library.

When a complete list of the population in a community is not available, the telephone book is probably the most obvious substitute for a sampling frame. This substitute is particularly attractive for telephone surveys. The researcher may claim that a random sample of the residents is accomplished by taking a random sample of the telephone numbers. The problem in this sampling method is that it ignores people without a phone or who have unlisted their phone numbers. The former are often the poor people and the latter either rich people or people in special situations such as battered spouses in hiding, so that the exclusion of people is not random in nature. A modified method of using the phone number is to let a computer generate four digit random numbers, then add this random number to a valid exchange number (the first three digits of a phone number in North America) to create a phone number. If this is not a valid phone number then this number plus one will be tried until a valid number is reached. Using this method, people who have unlisted phone numbers will also be included. Years ago a public library in Ontario, Canada used this sampling method to conduct a survey. Although this method is still imperfect because people who do not have a phone are excluded, it is better than using a phone book directly. It is definitely a better method than sampling users in the library on particular days. In the absence of a perfect sampling method, we often have to settle for the second best method. The design of a sampling method boils down to a battle against bias. You can use whatever creative method you can think of as long as it is unbiased. In choosing a sampling method we should also consider efficiency, cost, and practicality.

CHAPTER 7

Examining Relationships for Nominal and Ordinal Data— Chi-Square Test

The chi-square (also spelled as "χ^2") test is an inferential statistical test that is used to examine relationships between two variables with nominal or ordinal data. Perhaps it is the Greek letter in the name of this test that makes this lovely test (I will prove the loveliness in a minute) sound difficult and scary. I often hear people quoting this Greek-sounding test when they talk about the "foreign" nature of statistics and their fear of statistics. Ironically, the chi-square test is the most understandable among all the statistical tests. The formula to calculate the chi-square score is the simplest if you insist on doing manual calculations (of course, most people would not want to do so). The chi-square test is also the most useful test for analyzing data from surveys, which are often ordinal or nominal data. This combination of simplicity and applicability to common situations is the reason that I called it a "lovely test" at the beginning of this paragraph. It is also the reason that I have chosen the chi-square test as the first inferential statistical test to introduce, since it will convince you that inferential statistics is really not that difficult to understand and is very relevant to daily life. I will prove this point by starting with a simple example.

7.1 The Logic of the Chi-Square Test

Suppose that a community information center surveyed its users on their need for staff help in searching for information. One of the questions asked in the survey was whether the respondent sought staff help the last time he or she searched for information in the center. Answers to this question from 100 respondents, 50 males and 50 females, are summarized in Table 7-1.[1]

Table 7-1   Gender Breakdown in Seeking Staff Help

	Yes (sought staff help)	No (did not seek staff help)	Total
Male	5	45	50
Female	25	25	50
Total	30	70	100

Table 7-1 shows that 50 percent of females (25/50) sought help while only 10 percent of males (5/50) did so. If I ask you "Is there a relationship between gender and the tendency to seek staff help?" and, if yes, "Which gender group is more likely to seek help?" you will no doubt answer "Yes. Women are more likely to seek staff help." How did you reach this conclusion? Your reasoning is that if there is no relationship between the two variables, then men and women are equally likely to seek help and the percentage of men who sought help should be similar to that of women. Since there are equal numbers of men and women in the study, there should be equal numbers of men and women seeking help. So the 30 people seeking help should be equally distributed into the two gender groups; i.e., 15 in each as shown in Table 7-2. The same applies to the "no" category where men and women should have equal representation, also as shown in Table 7-2.

Table 7-2   Expected Gender Breakdown in Seeking Staff Help

	Yes (sought staff help)	No (did not seek staff help)	Total
Male	15	35	50
Female	15	35	50
Total	30	70	100

Because the data we collected (Table 7-1) deviate quite far from what we would expect if there were no relationship between the two variables (Table 7-2), the two variables must be related. The logic you used to reach this conclusion is exactly the same as that underlying the chi-square test. If we do a chi-square test on the data collected, we will reach the exact same conclusion. So the logic and the meaning of the chi-square test is really very straightforward. This may lead you to ask, "Why would we need a chi-square test if we can just look at the data and reach a conclusion by instinct?" The answer is that the above example is an extreme case of a very strong relationship between two variables. In reality, the relationship between the two variables may not be very strong so that the discrepancy between the data we collect and what we would expect may not be as large or as obvious as that between Table 7-1 and Table 7-2. To complicate things even further, there are often more than two categories (rows and/or columns) for each variable. For example, if the two variables being studied are occupation and the type of car owned, each variable has many possible categories. In such situations, it is difficult or even impossible to reach a definite conclusion just by looking at the tables. A chi-square test will provide an answer for us. Furthermore, the test, like any other statistical test, will tell us the probability for our conclusion to be correct, allowing us to state how certain we are of our conclusion.

We need to define a few terms before we can start a detailed discussion of the chi-square test. The cross tabulation of two variables as shown in Tables 7-1 and 7-2 is called a contingency table. Table 7-1 shows what we observed in data collection so it is called the observed table. The number in each cell of the observed table is called the observed frequency (f_o) because it is the frequency with which this particular category is observed in the data collected. For instance, $f_o = 5$ for the "male" and "yes" category in Table 7-1, which means that we observed five men who answered "yes" to the survey question about seeking help. In contrast, Table 7-2 is called the expected table and the number in each cell of an expected table is called the expected frequency (f_e). Expected frequency is the theoretical frequency we would expect to see if the two variables are not related.

The process for a chi-square test follows the general procedure for hypothesis testing outlined in Section 5.9 of Chapter 5. First, set up two competing hypotheses (Step 1 in Section 5.9). The null hypothesis assumes that there is no relationship between the two variables being studied and the alternative hypothesis states that the two variables are related. Next, calculate the test statistic, which is the chi-square score (Step 2). The chi-square score summarizes the discrepancies between the observed and the expected frequencies (details of the calculation will be discussed later). Third, determine the probability that the null hypothesis is true (the p-value) based on the test statistic (Step 3). The larger the chi-square score, the smaller the probability that the null hypothesis is true. Finally, compare the p-value to the pre-set significance level, usually 0.05, and reject the null hypothesis if the p-value is equal to or less than the pre-set level (Step 4). If a relationship is established (i.e., we reject the null hypothesis), we must then examine the data more closely to determine the exact pattern of the relationship (e.g., for the data in Table 7-1, the pattern is that women ask for help more often than men). In the next few sections, I will discuss each step of the process in detail.

7.2 Calculation of Expected Frequencies

Once we have established our hypotheses, the first thing we do in a chi-square test is to calculate the expected frequencies. Some software packages, such as SPSS, will calculate the expected frequencies as part of the chi-square test. Others, such as Excel, will not do this. In Excel, you have to enter the formula for the expected frequencies and then use the spreadsheet function to calculate the frequencies. Therefore, it is necessary to discuss the formula for calculating the expected frequencies.

For a small contingency table (fewer cells) with simple numbers, it is not difficult to determine the expected frequencies without a formula. For example, we had no difficulty in calculating Table 7-2 based on Table 7-1, since the 100 subjects in the study were equally divided between males and females. However, the numbers in the observed table are not always so "nice and neat." This makes it difficult to figure out the expected frequencies without using a formula. Table 7-3 gives an example of this kind of situation.

Table 7-3   A Hypothetical Table

	Yes (sought staff help)	No (did not seek staff help)	Total
Male	4	31	35
Female	39	24	63
Total	43	55	98

Although the numbers in Table 7-3 are not as "neat" as those in Table 7-1, the logic we will use to determine the expected frequencies is the same. If the two variables are not related so that males and females are equally likely to seek help, then the 43 "yes" people should be proportionally distributed between the two gender groups.

In other words, if x percent of the subjects are male, then x percent of the "yes" group should be male. Since 35.7 percent people in the study are males (35 males/98 subjects = 0.357), then there should be 15 males in the "yes" group (43 "yes" × 35.7 percent = 15, rounded to the nearest integer). The calculation of this "male" and "yes" expected frequency can be summarized as $\frac{35}{98}$ x 43 which, in mathematics, is the same as $\frac{35 \times 43}{98}$. If we call "35" the row marginal total of the cell, "43" the column marginal total, and "98" the grand total, then the formula to calculate the expected frequency of the cell can be generalized as:

(row marginal total × column marginal total) / grand total

This is the formula to calculate the expected frequency for any cell. For instance, to calculate the expected frequency for the "male" and "no" cell, just plug the following numbers into the formula: row marginal total = 35 (number of males); column marginal total = 55 (number of "no" responses); grand total = 98. The resulting expected frequency is 20 ($\frac{35 \times 55}{98}$, rounded to the nearest integer). Similarly, the two expected frequencies for the female row will be calculated at 28 for "yes" and 35 for "no." The four expected frequencies are shown in Table 7-4. The marginal totals and the grand total of the expected frequency table should add up to be the same as those in the observed table, as is the case in Table 7-3 and Table 7-4. If they are not the same, then there is a mistake in the calculation of the expected frequencies. While the observed frequencies are always integers, the expected frequencies can have decimals because of the way they are calculated. I rounded all the expected frequencies to integers in the above calculation for the convenience of discussion. It is not necessary to do so. In fact, leaving decimal points in the expected frequencies will actually result in a more accurate chi-square score.

Table 7-4 The Expected Frequencies for Table 7-3

	Yes (sought staff help)	No (did not seek staff help)	Total
Male	15	20	35
Female	28	35	63
Total	43	55	98

7.3 Chi-Square Score

Once we have calculated the expected frequencies for all cells, we can then calculate the chi-square score. The chi-square score is used to measure the discrepancy between the observed table and the expected table. It does so by calculating the discrepancy between the observed frequency and the corresponding expected frequency in each cell and then adding together the discrepancy figures for all the cells. To illustrate, let us use the example data in Table 7-1. Recall that Table 7-2 shows the corresponding expected frequencies for Table 7-1. The chi-square score (x^2) will be calculated as:

$$x^2 = \frac{(5-15)^2}{15} + \frac{(45-35)^2}{35} + \frac{(25-15)^2}{15} + \frac{(25-35)^2}{35} = 19.04$$

The four items in the above equation represent the discrepancies for the four cells of the contingency table. Let me explain why the discrepancy is calculated this way. The first item $(5-15)^2/15$ calculates the chi-square score for the "male" and "yes" cell. The difference between the observed frequency of 5 and the expected frequency of 15 is -10. The difference between the observed and the expected frequencies for the cell "male" and "no" (the second item in the above equation) is 10 (45-35). If we just add all the difference figures together, we will get zero for the chi-square score because the positives and negatives will cancel each other out. Therefore, we square each difference figure to cancel the negative signs and thus avoid summing to zero.

We then divide the squared difference by the expected frequency for the corresponding cell to put the differences on to a relative scale. This is done because the same difference score may be relatively larger or smaller depending on the size of the expected frequencies. A difference of 10 would be considered a small difference if the expected frequency were 1,000 but a large one if the expected frequency were 20. This is the same principle as using per capita measures to compare funding of different public libraries. Only when we divide funding by the population served can we meaningfully compare the funding levels of different libraries.

The above chi-square calculation can be summarized into a mathematical formula, which can be applied to contingency tables with any number of cells:

$$x^2 = \sum \frac{(f_o - f_e)^2}{f_e}$$

Here f_o stands for observed frequency and f_e represents the expected frequency. The Σ sign means summation; i.e., add together the discrepancies for all the cells. As usual, we do not have to worry about how to apply this formula and carry out the tedious calculation. Any statistical software can do it for us in seconds. We just have to know that the chi-square score measures the discrepancy between the observed frequencies and the expected frequencies. The larger the chi-square score, the larger the discrepancy, and the more likely it is that the two variables being studied are related. Recall that the null hypothesis assumes no relationship between the two variables. Therefore, the larger the chi-square score, the smaller the probability for the null hypothesis to be true. When this probability (the p-value) is equal to or smaller than a pre-set value, usually 0.05, we will reject the null hypothesis and conclude that the relationship between the two variables is statistically significant; i.e., there is a real relationship in the population, not just a chance relationship in the sample.

7.4 Chi-Square Table

Now that we have calculated the chi-square score, we can use it to determine the probability that the null hypothesis is true (the p-value). There is a mathematical formula to calculate the p-values for various chi-square scores with various sizes of contingency tables. The good news is that we do not have to calculate this probability ourselves. What we really need to know is whether or not the p-value associated with this chi-square score is less than the pre-set level, usually 0.05. We can easily find this out by checking a table called the table of the critical values of chi-square (chi-square table for short) shown in Appendix 3. The "critical value" is the value of the test statistic at which the p-value is at a pre-set level. The statistical term "critical value" is similar to "threshold value" in our daily language. When the calculated chi-square score is equal to or greater than the "critical value" listed in the chi-square table, the p-value is at or less than the pre-set level, so we can reject the null hypothesis. On the other hand, if the calculated chi-square score is less than the "critical value," then the p-value is greater than the pre-set level and we will fail to reject the null hypothesis. The next question is how we locate the critical value in the chi-square table for the specific contingency table we are dealing with. I have reproduced part of the Appendix 3 as Table 7-5 for the convenience of discussion.

Table 7-5   Critical Values of Chi-Square for df Between 1 and 4

df	0.05	0.01
1	3.84	6.63
2	5.99	9.21
3	7.81	11.34
4	9.49	13.28

The first column of Table 7-5 is df, which stands for degrees of freedom. It is a statistical term associated with every statistical test and its specific meaning varies from test to test. In the case of the chi-square test, it means the number of cells whose cell frequencies are free to change once the row marginal totals and the column marginal totals are fixed. To illustrate, let us look at Table 7-1 again. Once we fix the values of all the row and column marginal totals (50, 50, 30, 70) and one of the cell frequencies, then figures in all the other cells are not free to change anymore because of the constraint of adding up to the row and column marginal totals. For instance, if you fix the value in the "male" and "yes" cell to be 5, then the "male" and "no" cell must be 45 in order to add up to the row marginal total of 50. By the same token, the "female" and "yes" cell must be 25 in order for the column marginal total to be 30. The "female" and "no" cell can only be 25 now to add up to the right marginal totals.

So there is only one cell that is free to change its frequency in this 2 by 2 table (2 by 2 means that there are two categories for each variable). Indeed, this is true for any 2 by 2 table. Thus the degrees of freedom for a 2 by 2 table is 1. The degrees of freedom for a 2 by 3 table is 2 because if you fix the row marginal totals and column marginal totals and any of the two cell frequencies there, no other cell frequencies are free to change (I suggest that you try this out in a table with 2 rows and 3 columns or 3 rows and 2 columns). In general, the degrees of freedom for any contingency table can be calculated as:

df = (number of rows –1) × (number of columns –1)

So for a table with 5 rows and 4 columns, the degrees of freedom is 12 ((5-1) × (4-1) = 4 × 3 = 12).

The second column of Table 7-5 lists critical values of chi-square for a p-value of 0.05. This 0.05 is also called the significance level or α level. The third column of Table 7-5 lists critical values of chi-square for significance level of 0.01. To locate a critical value in Table 7-5, first determine df, as discussed above, and then look across to the column with the desired significance level. For example, if df for the contingency table is 2, then the critical value is 5.99 for significance level of 0.05 and 9.21 for significance level of 0.01. Table 7-5 shows that for a given significance level, the critical value increases as df increases. This is because a larger df means a larger contingency table (with more cells). The more cells there are, the greater the chi-square score can potentially be. (Recall that the chi-square score is calculated by adding together the discrepancies between the observed and expected frequencies for all the cells.) The degrees of freedom is used to account for this fact and adjust the critical value accordingly.

Usually we use a significance level of 0.05; i.e., we will reject the null hypothesis if the probability for it to be true is equal to or less than 0.05. For the example data we have been working with in Table 7-1, the df is 1, so the critical value is 3.84. Since our calculated chi-square score of 19.04 (see the calculation result in the first paragraph of Section 7.3) is greater than the critical value, we reject the null hypothesis and conclude that there is a relationship between gender and seeking staff help. Now that we know that males and females have different tendencies to seek staff help, we will want to know if males or females are more likely to seek help. This is called the pattern of the relationship. In general, once we know that two variables are related, we always need to determine the pattern of the relationship to gain more information from the data collected and make our investigation complete.

7.5 Examining the Pattern of the Relationship

The pattern of the relationship between two variables can be determined by comparing the observed frequencies to the expected frequencies. I will continue our discussion of the data on gender and seeking staff help to explain how to do this. I have combined Table 7-1 (observed frequencies) and Table 7-2 (expected frequencies) into a single table as shown in Table 7-6 to make it easier to do the comparison. There are two numbers in each cell of Table 7-6.

The first is the observed frequency and the second, shown in brackets, is the expected frequency.

Table 7-6 Comparing Observed Frequencies to Expected Frequencies

	Yes (sought staff help)	No (did not seek staff help)	Total
Male	5 (15)	45 (35)	50
Female	25 (15)	25 (35)	50
Total	30	70	100

Note: Numbers within brackets are the expected frequencies.

We can select either the "yes" column or the "no" column to start examining the pattern. Let us begin with the "yes" column. The expected frequency in the "yes" and "male" cell tells us that if there were no relationship between the two variables (i.e., males and females were equally likely to seek staff help) we would expect that 15 out of the 50 males would have sought help. However only five of them did so. This means that males are less inclined to seek staff help. On the other hand, the numbers in the "yes" and "female" cell tell us that 25 females sought help, more than the 15 we would expect if there were no relationship between gender and seeking help. Therefore, the conclusion is that females are more likely than males to seek help. If you examine the two cells in the "no" column, you will reach the same conclusion. This is guaranteed as long as the expected frequencies are calculated correctly. If males are under-represented in the "yes" side, then they will be over-represented in the "no" side.

7.6 An Example of Using Software to Carry Out a Chi-Square Test

Now that we have discussed the different components of a chi-square test, I will demonstrate the complete process of the test by analyzing a real data set using SPSS. The data come from a research project investigating the information search patterns of business communities (Vaughan, 1997). Two surveys, one aimed at small business and the other at medium-sized business, were carried out. Use of various information sources, especially the public library, for business purposes was examined. To assess the importance of the public library to the business community, one of the questions asked in both surveys was "What would be the impact on your business of closing the library?" (The library here refers to the local public library.) Answers to the question were classified into four categories: no impact, minimal impact, some impact, and significant impact. The research question was whether the impact level would be the same for both small and medium-sized businesses. Another way of stating the question is whether the impact level would be related to the business size. A chi-square test was used to answer the question. The null hypothesis for this chi-square test is that there is no relationship between the size of the business and the impact level. Note that the null hypothesis always assumes that there is no relationship even if the purpose of the study is to prove that the two variables are related. In other words, the research hypothesis (what we speculate to be true) and the statistical hypothesis (the null hypothesis) can be, and often are, different. When these two hypotheses are opposite, we can prove our research hypothesis by rejecting the null hypothesis (i.e., proving that the null hypothesis is wrong).

There are two variables here: the size of the business and the impact level. For entry into SPSS, we have to code both variables using numbers. Business size was coded as 1 for small businesses and 2 for medium-sized businesses. The four impact levels were coded from 1, no impact, to 4, significant impact. The original data collected were entered into SPSS in two columns (not in a contingency table form directly) as shown below:

Size	Impact
1	2
2	3
1	4
2	2
.	.
.	.

A total of 293 businesses participated in the study; i.e., there were 293 data points. There is no need for us to manually tabulate these 293 data points into a contingency table, which would be very time-consuming. SPSS will create the contingency table as part of the chi-square test. After inputting the data into SPSS, I went through menu options of "Analyze," "Descriptive Statistics," and "Crosstabs." I then specified "impact" as the row and "size" as the column for the crosstab ("crosstab" stands for cross tabulation; i.e., the contingency table). I also specified chi-square as the required statistics. The SPSS output is as shown in Figure 7-1.

Case Processing Summary

	Cases					
	Valid		Missing		Total	
	N	Percent	N	Percent	N	Percent
IMPACT * SIZE	232	79.2%	61	20.8%	293	100.0%

IMPACT * SIZE Crosstabulation

			SIZE		
			small business	medium sized business	Total
IMPACT	no impact	Count	61	42	103
		Expected Count	59.9	43.1	103.0
	minimal impact	Count	33	25	58
		Expected Count	33.8	24.3	58.0
	some impact	Count	9	21	30
		Expected Count	17.5	12.5	30.0
	significant impact	Count	32	9	41
		Expected Count	23.9	17.1	41.0
Total		Count	135	97	232
		Expected Count	135.0	97.0	232.0

Chi-Square Tests

	Value	df	Asymp. Sig. (2-sided)
Pearson Chi-Square	16.530[a]	3	.001
Likelihood Ratio	16.999	3	.001
Linear-by-Linear Association	.631	1	.427
N of Valid Cases	232		

a. 0 cells (.0%) have expected count less than 5. The minimum expected count is 12.54.

Figure 7-1   SPSS Output for the Chi-Square Test

The SPSS output consists of three tables. The first one is the case processing summary, which tells us the number and the percent of valid cases and missing cases. There were 293 businesses in this study (shown as the total number of cases in the output). Sixty-one of them did not answer the impact question (shown as number of missing cases). The remaining 232 responses were used in the chi-square test (shown as the number of valid cases). The second table in Fig. 7-1 is the contingency table for the chi-square test. There are two numbers in each cell. The first one, shown as "Count," is the observed frequency and the second one, shown as "Expected Count," is the expected frequency. The last table in Figure 7-1 is the chi-square test result.

There are different types of chi-square test with different ways of calculating the chi-square score. The table displays a few of them. The one we are discussing in this book is the Pearson chi-square test, which is the most commonly used type of chi-square test. It is displayed in the first row of the last table in Figure 7-1. I have bolded this row for the convenience of discussion. The first column of the table is the name of the test, the second is the chi-square score, the next is the degrees of freedom, and the last is the p-value. The small print at the bottom of Figure 7-1 warns of the number of cells with expected frequencies under five. In this case there are no such cells. The issue of having expected frequencies under five will be discussed in the next section.

SPSS calculated the Pearson chi-square score at 16.53 and the degrees of freedom at 3. The p-value for this chi-square score is 0.001. This means that, based on the data we collected, the probability for the null hypothesis to be true is only 0.001. Since this is less than the usual 0.05 level, we reject the null hypothesis and conclude that the impact level is related to business size. Some software may only provide the chi-square score without giving the associated p-value as SPSS does. If this is the case, you just have to check the chi-square table to find out if the p-value is greater than or less than 0.05 as we discussed in Section 7.4.

Now that we know there is a relationship between business size and the impact level, we need to find out the pattern of the relationship; i.e., whether the small businesses or medium-sized businesses are more likely to be affected by closing the library. This question can be answered by comparing the observed vs. expected frequencies in the second table of Figure 7-1. It is clear that the observed frequencies and the expected frequencies are fairly close in the "no impact" or "minimal impact" categories, while there is an obvious discrepancy between the two frequencies in the "some impact" and "significant impact" categories. Relatively more small businesses fall into the "significant impact" category (observed frequency greater than the expected frequency) while more medium-sized businesses fall into the "some impact" group. Therefore, we can conclude that the absence of public libraries would have a more significant impact on small businesses than on medium-sized businesses, although there would also be some impact on the latter.

It is always a good idea to provide more information from the data by reporting the row or column percentage of a contingency table. In this case, it is useful to report the percent of businesses in the four impact rows; i.e., what percent of businesses will be affected by the closing of the public library. A quick calculation shows that the percent of businesses in the four impact groups (from no impact to significant impact) are 44 percent (103/232), 25 percent, 13 percent, and 18 percent respectively (it is also possible to have SPSS include the percentages when it generates the table). It may be disappointing to see that closing the public library would have no impact on over 40 percent of the businesses surveyed. It is also important to notice that closing the public library would have some or even significant impact on 31 percent of the businesses, both small and medium-sized. If there are 1,000 businesses in the community, 310 of them will be affected by the closing of the library, a significant impact on the community indeed.

I would like to add a quick note on the selection of software for doing the chi-square test. Excel is not a recommended choice for this test. SPSS only requires a few mouse clicks to get a complete chi-square test result as demonstrated in the above example. By contrast, Excel requires several steps including inputting the formula to calculate expected frequencies. A mistake in inputting the formula will cause the test result to be wrong. In my years of experience teaching statistics, I found beginners have great difficulty doing chi-square tests using Excel.

7.7 Requirements for Using Chi-Square Test

All inferential statistical tests have certain requirements on the data and the chi-square test is no exception. The following four requirements must be satisfied before a chi-square test can be performed:

- The sample must be randomly selected.
- The data must be of nominal or ordinal type.
- Cell entries must be independent of each other.
- Expected frequencies should be large enough.

The first requirement only means that the sample cannot be biased. It does not exclude the use of systemic or stratified samples. As we discussed in Chapter 6, a biased sample will lead to biased conclusions. The reason for the second requirement is obvious: only nominal or ordinal data can be tabulated into a contingency table. If the data are in interval or ratio form, do not convert them into nominal or ordinal form to be analyzed by a chi-square test. The conversion will lose information contained in the data as was discussed in Section 1.5 of Chapter 1. We have other statistical tests, to be discussed in later chapters, which can be applied to interval or ratio data.

To explain the third requirement, let us look at Table 7-1 again. People in all four cells should be independent of each other. If the five males in the "yes" cell are in some way related to the 25 females in the "yes" cell (for instance, the five males taught the 25 females how to use this information center so that the males and females' search behaviors, including their tendency to seek staff help, are not independent of each other), then the chi-square test cannot be applied to this data set.

The fourth requirement stems from the fact that the chi-square score is sensitive to the effect of small expected frequencies (i.e., the chi-square score may be exaggerated by small expected frequencies). How small is small enough to cause the problem? There is no hard-and-fast rule on the issue. Different books give somewhat different rules. For example, the criteria given by Sprinthall (1997, 332-333) and Erickson and Nosanchuk (1992, 251) are different, but they all aim at expected frequencies being large enough. A guideline that many researchers use and that I will use in this book is (1) no cell has an expected frequency of less than 1; and (2) not more than 20 percent of the cells have expected frequencies of less than five (SPSS Inc., 1998, 67, Diekhoff, 1996, 212). SPSS also lists these criteria under its help topic "Chi-Square Test, assumptions." What can we do if the expected frequencies are not large enough to meet the above criteria? I will use an example to explain how to deal with this problem. In the previous section, we discussed the study of the impact of closing the public library on business communities. Suppose that there were only 90 rather than 293 businesses participating in the study and the chi-square test result is as shown in Figure 7-2.

As is warned at the end of the SPSS output, 25 percent of the cells have expected frequencies under five so that the fourth requirement for the chi-square test is not met. An examination of the contingency table (second table in Figure 7-2) shows that the two cells with low expected frequencies are in the "minimal impact" row. If we collapse the table by merging this row with another row, then the expected frequencies may all be greater than five. The choice of which row to

Case Processing Summary

	Cases					
	Valid		Missing		Total	
	N	Percent	N	Percent	N	Percent
IMPACT * SIZE	90	100.0%	0	.0%	90	100.0%

IMPACT * SIZE Crosstabulation

			SIZE		
			small business	medium sized business	Total
IMPACT	no impact	Count	6	6	12
		Expected Count	6.7	5.3	12.0
	minimal impact	Count	3	4	7
		Expected Count	3.9	3.1	7.0
	some impact	Count	9	21	30
		Expected Count	16.7	13.3	30.0
	significant impact	Count	32	9	41
		Expected Count	22.8	18.2	41.0
Total		Count	50	40	90
		Expected Count	50.0	40.0	90.0

Chi-Square Tests

	Value	df	Asymp. Sig. (2-sided)
Pearson Chi-Square	16.943[a]	3	.001
Likelihood Ratio	17.649	3	.001
Linear-by-Linear Association	5.528	1	.019
N of Valid Cases	90		

a. 2 cells (25.0%) have expected count less than 5. The minimum expected count is 3.11.

Figure 7-2   An Example of Expected Frequencies Not Being Large Enough

merge with is not a completely arbitrary decision. The newly merged row must be meaningful. A merger of the "minimal impact" row with the "significant impact" row will result in a meaningless row; i.e., it would be difficult to interpret what it means. The best choice in this case is to merge the "minimal impact" row with the "no impact" row to form a new row called "no impact or minimal impact."

Originally, the "no impact" category was coded as "1" and the "minimal impact" category coded as "2." To implement the merger, we will have to recode these two categories either in a new code such as "5" or an existing code such as "1." I chose the latter and called the newly coded variable "recoded impact." To implement this recode in

SPSS, go through the menu options "Transform," "Recode," "Into Different Variables," and then specify the old and the new codes. I conducted a chi-square test on the newly coded data and the result is shown in Figure 7-3.

Case Processing Summary

	Cases					
	Valid		Missing		Total	
	N	Percent	N	Percent	N	Percent
recoded impact * SIZE	90	100.0%	0	.0%	90	100.0%

recoded impact * SIZE Crosstabulation

			SIZE		
			small business	medium sized business	Total
recoded impact	no or minimal impact	Count	9	10	19
		Expected Count	10.6	8.4	19.0
	some impact	Count	9	21	30
		Expected Count	16.7	13.3	30.0
	significant impact	Count	32	9	41
		Expected Count	22.8	18.2	41.0
Total		Count	50	40	90
		Expected Count	50.0	40.0	90.0

Chi-Square Tests

	Value	df	Asymp. Sig. (2-sided)
Pearson Chi-Square	16.852[a]	2	.000
Likelihood Ratio	17.559	2	.000
Linear-by-Linear Association	5.211	1	.022
N of Valid Cases	90		

a. 0 cells (.0%) have expected count less than 5. The minimum expected count is 8.44.

Figure 7-3 Data in Figure 7-2 Recoded

After recoding, none of the expected frequencies is under five so the fourth requirement for the chi-square test is met. Notice that the contingency table size is now 3 by 2 rather than the original 4 by 2, and the degrees of freedom is reduced from 3 to 2 accordingly.

Endnote

1. These numbers are made up for the convenience of discussion. They are not meant to reflect the real information search behavior of men and women. Also note that not seeking staff help does not mean that there is no need for staff help, only that the respondent did not ask for help.

CHAPTER 8

Examining Relationships for Interval and Ratio Data— Correlation and Regression

The terms correlation and regression may sound like statistical jargon to most people but we actually encounter the concepts in daily life. We may even apply the concepts although we may not be consciously aware of it or view it in statistical terms. For instance, we know that a baby's body grows bigger with age. To state this in statistical terms, we say that there is a positive correlation between a baby's body size and age. Because of this correlation, the baby clothing industry and parents estimate a baby's size based on age. Therefore, baby clothes are often labeled by age. In statistical terms, what we are doing here is regression. That is, we work out a quantitative relationship between two variables and then use that knowledge to predict one variable (body size) based on the other variable (age).

Of course, there are exceptions to this general rule of size and age. Not all babies grow at the same rate, nor are all babies of the same age the same size. Statistically speaking, we say that the correlation between age and size is not perfect or even very strong. In fact, statistical correlation addresses the issues of the strength, the type, and the statistical significance of the relationship. If we detect a significant relationship between two variables, we can then use regression analysis to develop a mathematical equation to describe the relationship quantitatively. The regression equation will also allow us to predict one variable based on the other. We can even know the accuracy of this prediction based on the strength of the correlation. In this chapter, we will first discuss correlation, including the basic concept, the measurement, and the significance testing of correlation, and then go on to regression, including regression equation, regression line, and prediction.

8.1   Types of Correlation

The correlation between a baby's size and age mentioned above is a positive correlation. In a positive correlation, the value of one variable increases as the value of the other variable increases. There are many examples of positive correlation in daily life; e.g., the taller a person is, the heavier he/she may be. In library and information science, we know that there is a relationship between the size of a library's collection and the library's circulation. The larger the collection, the larger the circulation. A positive relationship can be characterized by the statement "the more… the more…," e.g., the more the collection, the more the circulation.

I found that people usually do not have a problem understanding the positive correlation. However, some beginners have trouble with another type of correlation, the negative correlation. They think that negative correlation means no relationship when, in fact, it means a relationship where the value of one variable decreases as the value of the other variable increases. As with positive correlation, we can find many examples of negative correlation in daily life. Imagine that you are driving to a place that is a certain distance away and you start timing the trip as you leave. The more time you spend driving, the shorter the distance left. So there is a negative relationship between the variables "time spent on driving" and "distance left." Negative relationships can be characterized by the statement "the more… the less…," e.g., the more time spent on driving, the less distance left. One of the best examples of negative correlation in information science is the inverse relationship between recall and precision in information retrieval. Usually, when recall increases, precision decreases, and vice versa.

There are, of course, many examples in which two variables are not related. There is no relationship between people's height and their intelligence. Nor is there a relationship between an information professional's weight and the ability of the professional to find information. In these situations, we say that the two variables are not correlated. The difference between negative correlation and no correlation should be clear now. The former has a pattern between the two variables and we can predict one variable based on the other while the latter has no pattern at all.

8.2 Using A Scatter Plot to View the Pattern of Relationship

When we collect data to study the relationship between two variables, we must collect and store the data in pairs. For example, if we are studying the relationship between recall and precision and conduct 18 searches with various search strategies and search tasks, we should calculate recall and precision figures for each of these 18 searches and store the figures in pairs such as the following:

Table 8-1 Recall and Precision Data

Recall	0.15	0.2	0.23	0.27	0.7	0.35	0.4	0.45	0.55
Precision	0.7	0.65	0.6	0.5	0.3	0.4	0.36	0.3	0.28
Recall	0.6	0.2	0.8	0.4	0.8	0.55	0.4	0.2	0.1
Precision	0.2	0.7	0.2	0.5	0.1	0.4	0.3	0.5	0.6

The first recall figure matches the first precision figure and they are the result of the first search. The same applies to the remaining pairs. We can now plot these 18 pairs of data into a two dimensional graph with each pair of data being represented by a dot on the graph as shown in Figure 8-1 (try to locate a few pairs of data to see how the graph is generated). This graph is called a scatter plot. It is obtained through Excel 2000 by going through menu options "Insert," "Chart," "XY (Scatter)," and then providing various graph specifications as prompted.

A scatter plot is a very useful tool in studying a correlation. It not only provides us with a first impression as to whether or not there is a relationship but also indicates the type of relationship (i.e., positive or negative). If the data points show a downward trend, as in Figure 8-1, then it is a negative relationship. An upward trend, as shown in Figure 8-2, signals a positive relationship. If there is no clear pattern, as in the case of Figure 8-3, then there is no relationship between the two variables.

8.3 Measuring the Strength of a Relationship—Pearson r

When two variables are related, we can predict one variable based on the other. But the accuracy of the prediction varies in different

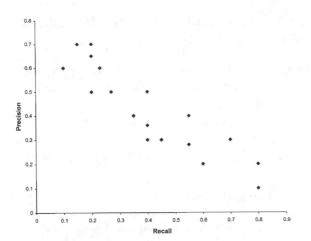

Figure 8-1 A Scatter Plot Showing a Negative Relationship

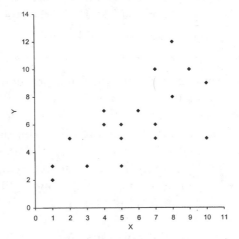

Figure 8-2 A Scatter Plot Showing a Positive Relationship

situations. For example, prediction of people's weight based on their height will be less accurate than prediction of the distance traveled based on the time spent driving at a constant speed. There are many factors that influence a person's weight other than height, such as diet, exercise, etc. By contrast, if you are driving at a constant speed, the distance traveled on a highway depends mainly on the time spent on driving. In statistical terms, we say that the latter case has a stronger relationship than the former. In order to give a better description of a relationship, we need a measurement to indicate its strength. The correlation coefficient is designed for this purpose.

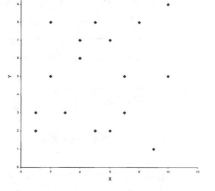

Figure 8-3 A Scatter Plot Showing No Relationship

Specifically, we use the Pearson correlation coefficient, symbolized by r_p, to measure the strength of relationships for interval and ratio data. In Chapter 11, we will encounter the Spearman correlation coefficient, r_s, which is used to measure the strength of relationships for ordinal data.

If the two variables being studied are represented by X and Y respectively, then Pearson r_p is defined as:

$$r_p = \frac{\sum z_x z_y}{N}$$

where z_x and z_y are the Z scores (see Chapter 5) of the variables X and Y respectively. There are various other formulae for calculating the Pearson r and they are derived from this formula. As usual, we can let computer software calculate r_p for us instead of dealing with the formula ourselves.

To give a sense of what kind of numbers we will get for the Pearson correlation coefficient, I will use Excel to calculate r_p for the three sets of data in Figure 8-1 to 8-3.

The menu options to go through in Excel to calculate r_p are "Tools," "Data Analysis," "Correlation," and then specify input range (where the data to be analyzed are located) and output range (where the result should go). The resulting r_p for the data sets in Figure 8-1 to 8-3 are -0.9, 0.68, and 0.17 respectively. As an example of the Excel output for r_p, Figure 8-4 shows the Excel result for the recall and precision data in Figure 8-1. The output for r_p is shown in a table format. The r_p between recall and precision is -0.89918. The r_p

between recall and recall is 1 (the correlation of the variable to itself is always 1, i.e., 100 percent) as is the correlation between precision and precision.

	Recall	Precision
Recall	1	
Precision	-0.89918	1

Figure 8-4   Excel Output of r_p for Recall and Precision Data

The Pearson correlation coefficient ranges from -1 to 1. A negative number signals a negative relationship, a positive number signals a positive relationship, and numbers near zero mean no relationship. Remember that Figure 8-1 to 8-3 represent negative, positive, and no relationship respectively. The three r_p numbers confirm this fact. The absolute value of the Pearson correlation coefficient (i.e., the numeric value without considering positive and negative signs) indicates the strength of a relationship. The closer the absolute value of r_p is to 1, the stronger the relationship. The closer it is to zero, the weaker the relationship. A value that is close to zero indicates that there is no relationship. Because the absolute value of r_p for Figure 8-1 is 0.9, greater than the 0.68 for Figure 8-2, we can say that the variables in Figure 8-1 have a stronger relationship than those in Figure 8-2. A visual comparison of the two figures confirms this fact. While data points in both scatter plots resemble a straight line, those in Figure 8-1 fall closer to the line and those in Figure 8-2 are "looser" and scatter further away from the line. A perfect relationship where all data points fall exactly on a straight line will have a correlation coefficient of either positive 1 or negative 1 depending on the direction of the line.

8.4   Testing the Significance of Pearson r

We can determine whether or not two variables are related by using inferential statistics. To do this, we collect a sample of data and then generalize our conclusion from the sample to the population. We know that the larger the absolute value of r_p for the sample data, the stronger the relationship and more likely that there is a relationship in the population. How large does r_p have to be for us to confidently conclude a relationship? We have a statistical test to answer this question. This test is called the significance test of r_p.

The procedure for the significance test of Pearson r follows the general process of hypothesis testing outlined in Section 5.9 of Chapter 5. First, set up two competing hypotheses (Step 1 of the process). The null hypothesis assumes that there is no relationship between the two variables in the population and the alternative hypothesis states that the two variables are related. Next, calculate the test statistic, which is r_p, for the sample data (Step 2). Then, determine the probability of the null hypothesis being true (the p-value) based on the test statistic r_p (Step 3). The larger the absolute value of r_p the smaller the p-value. Finally, compare the p-value to a pre-set significance level, usually 0.05 (Step 4). If the p-value is equal to or less than the pre-set level, we will reject the null hypothesis and conclude that the relationship is statistically significant; i.e., that there is a real relationship between the two variables in the population. If the p-value is greater than 0.05, we will fail to reject the null hypothesis, meaning that we have insufficient evidence to say that the two variables are related in the population.

To determine the p-value based on the test statistic r_p, we will use a statistical table called the critical values of r_p, which is shown in Appendix 4. The statistical term "critical value" is similar to "threshold value" in our daily language. If the absolute value of the calculated r_p is equal to or greater than the critical value, then the p-value is equal to or less than the pre-set significance level and we will reject the null hypothesis. To locate a critical value in Appendix 4, we first need to determine the degrees of freedom (the columns labeled as df in Appendix 4), which is calculated as the number of pairs of data minus 2. Thus, if we have ten pairs of data, then df = 8 (10-2) and the corresponding critical value is 0.6319 for a significance level of 0.05 (look across the column labeled as 0.05). Similarly, for a significance level of 0.01, the critical value is 0.7646.

For a given significance level, the only thing that determines the critical value is the degrees of freedom, which is calculated based on the sample size. The larger the sample size (more pairs of data), the larger the degrees of freedom and, consequently, the smaller the critical value (as shown in Appendix 4, the critical value decreases as df increases). This makes sense when you consider the logic of this significance test. For a given correlation coefficient r_p, say 0.5, we will be more confident to conclude that there is a real relationship in the population if r_p is calculated from a larger sample size, say 30, than if it is from a small sample size, say 10. The larger critical value associated with the smaller sample size makes it less likely that we will reject the null hypothesis and conclude a relationship. So the df is really designed to take the sample size into consideration.

I will use an example to illustrate how to carry out a significance test of the correlation coefficient r_p. A survey was conducted to investigate the preparedness of Canadian federal depository libraries for the transition to electronic access to government information (Dolan and Vaughan, 1998). Two of the questions asked were about the number of employees and the number of PCs for staff use only. I want to determine if these two variables are related among all the government libraries (the population) from 37 such libraries participating in the study (the sample). The null hypothesis is that there is no relationship between the two variables. The Pearson correlation coefficient (r_p) calculated by Excel is 0.86. The degrees of freedom is 35 (there are 37 government libraries in the survey so there are 37 pairs of data). According to Appendix 4, the critical value is 0.3246 for the significance level of 0.05. Because our calculated r_p is 0.86, greater than the critical value, we reject the null hypothesis and conclude that the number of staff PCs is related to the number of employees.

As another example, let us look at Figure 8-3 again. There are 17 pairs of data so the df is 15. The Pearson correlation coefficient is calculated at 0.166, which is less than the critical value of 0.4821. Therefore we fail to reject the null hypothesis of no relationship. The fact that scatter plot shows no particular pattern of relationship echoes this conclusion.

8.5 Correlation and Causation

Once a correlation between two variables is established, it is tempting to state it as a causal relationship. This is a common mistake that people make when interpreting statistics. Correlation does not mean causation. First, a statistically significant correlation coefficient between variables X and Y, be it positive or negative, tells us nothing about whether X caused Y or Y caused X. Second, it is quite possible that neither X caused Y nor Y caused X but that a third variable, Z, is causing both X and Y to change in a related fashion.

Let us examine a couple of examples of correlation and causation. We know that there is a correlation between people's weight and height. But the correlation coefficient, say 0.6, tells us nothing about which variable caused the other. It is our knowledge of the variables that tells us that height caused weight and not the other way around; i.e., putting on more weight will not make one taller. Of course, height is not the only factor that affects weight, which is why the correlation coefficient between the two variables is not a perfect 1.

It has been found that the percentage of dropouts in each of a number of high schools is negatively correlated with the number of books per student in the libraries of those high schools (Hopkins and Glass, 1978, 145). Does the high dropout rate cause the smaller library holdings or vice versa? The chances are that neither caused the other. Common sense tells us that simply piling more books into the school library will not affect the dropout rates much, and lowering the dropout rates will not cause a larger library collection. The high dropout rates and the smaller library collection are probably both caused by a third variable; e.g., a hostile environment for education in those schools.

What does it mean, then, when we say that the correlation coefficient between X and Y is statistically significant? It means that there is a very good chance, at least 95 percent if we use the significance level of 0.05, that there is a real relationship between the two variables in the population, not just a coincidence in the sample. If the test of r_p fails to show that the relationship is statistically significant, i.e., we fail to reject the null hypothesis of no relationship, then it means that we have insufficient evidence to prove a relationship between the two variables in the population. In any case, there is nothing about the correlation test that identifies the relationship as a causal one. You might ask why we study the correlation if it does not tell us anything about causation? The answer is that the knowledge of a correlation will provide us with the ability to make a better-than-chance prediction about the variables. Specifically, we can use regression analysis to establish an equation that links the two variables quantitatively. We can then predict one variable based on the other using the regression equation. It should be noted that if a test of Pearson r fails to prove a significant relationship, then we should not proceed to develop a regression equation because it will be meaningless to describe a non-existing relationship through an equation.

Using regression analysis to develop equations and make predictions is the topic of the remaining part of this chapter.

8.6   Regression Equation and Regression Line

When two variables X and Y are related, as in Figure 8-5 (ignore the line on the scatter plot for the moment), we can predict one variable based on the other. For the two variables in Figure 8-5, if I ask you to predict the Y value for X equals 5, what would you say? A close look at the scatter plot reveals that corresponding to X = 5 there are three data points with three different Y values. Which Y value should you predict? The same dilemma applies to many other X values. The data points in the scatter plot do not exactly fall on a straight line but rather resemble the line by scattering around it. The solution to this problem in prediction is that we will figure out a straight line that "represents" all the data points and then do our prediction according to this line, i.e., let the predicted Y value fall on that line. This "representative" line is called the regression line and is defined as the single straight line that comes closest to all of the data points in the scatter plot. The line on Figure 8-5 is such a line. So we can predict that when X = 5, Y = 6.35, because the line passes through this point.

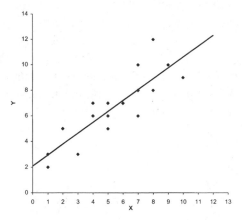

Figure 8-5   Illustration of a Regression Line

How do we figure out this line? We learned in high school mathematics that a straight line on a two-dimensional plane of X and Y can be described by an equation Y = a + bX. Any data point that satisfies this equation will fall on the line and any data point on the line will fit the equation. The two coefficients in the equation, a and b, uniquely define the line. Coefficient b is called the slope and represents the degree of steepness of the line. Coefficient a is the intercept, the point where the line crosses the Y axis.

Three lines are displayed in Figure 8-6 to illustrate the concepts of slope and intercept. The first line (counterclockwise direction) is represented by the equation Y = X which means that a = 0 and b = 1. Because a = 0, the line crosses the Y-axis at the zero point. The equation for the second line is Y = 2+X. The line crosses the Y-axis at 2 because a = 2. The line is parallel to the first line because both have a slope of 1 so that their steepness is the same. The third line, whose equation is Y = 2+2X, also crosses the Y-axis at 2, but it is steeper than the first two lines because its slope is larger.

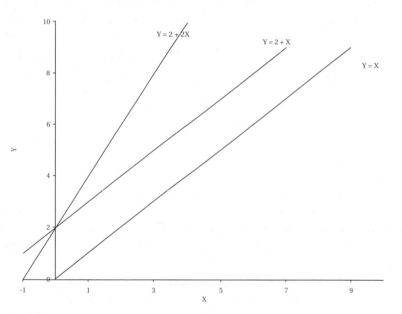

Figure 8-6 Illustration of Slope and Intercept

The question now is how to determine the values of the slope and intercept for the regression line so that the line comes closest to all the data points we have. We do not have to try different lines to look for the best one. If we use the following formulae to calculate coefficients a and b, we will get the line we are looking for.

$$b = \frac{rSD_y}{SD_x} \qquad a = \overline{Y} - b\overline{X}$$

Here, r is the Pearson correlation coefficient. SD_y means standard deviation of variable Y and SD_x is the standard deviation of variable X. $\overline{y}$ and $\overline{x}$ are the means of Y and X respectively. We have discussed how to use software to calculate all these numbers earlier in the book. If the software package that you are using has the regression analysis function, then you do not have to calculate these numbers first and then plug them into the above formulae to determine a and b. The software can calculate regression coefficients a and b directly and include them in the output of a regression analysis.

Before calculating regression coefficients a and b, either manually or using a software package, we first have to decide which variable is X (right side of the regression equation) and which one is Y (left side of the equation). The Y variable in regression analysis is called the dependent variable and the X variable, the independent variable. The terms "independent variable" and "dependent variable" are also used in textbooks on research methods where they have specific definitions. For the purpose of the regression equation, we can say that the dependent variable is the unknown variable that needs to be predicted and the independent variable is the known variable on which the prediction will be based. In a scatter plot, the X variable is always located on the horizontal axis and the Y variable always on the vertical axis.

For an example of developing a regression equation and a regression line, I will keep analyzing the data from the survey of Canadian federal depository libraries that we used in Section 4 of this chapter. In Section 4, we established that there is a positive correlation between the number of staff PCs and the number of employees. Therefore, we can develop a regression equation for these two variables. Suppose that I want to predict the number of staff PCs based on the number of employees. Staff PCs will then be the Y variable and number of employees will be the X variable. I used Excel to do the regression for this example. After going through menu options "Tools," "Data Analysis," "Regression," and then specifying X and Y variables, I got the output as shown in Figure 8-7.

The Excel output in Figure 8-7 consists of three parts. The first part, titled "regression statistics," includes the Pearson correlation coefficient, which is labeled as "Multiple R." The number shown here

(0.86) is identical to what we obtained earlier when we calculated the correlation coefficient (see second last paragraph of Section 4 of this chapter). The next line, "R Square," is the coefficient of determination, which will be discussed in the next section. The last line, "Observations," shows the number of data points involved in the regression analysis, 37. We will skip the third and fourth lines in the first part as well as the second part titled "ANOVA" because they are about topics that we do not discuss in this book. The last part of Figure 8-7 shows the regression coefficients (in the "Coefficients" column) and their related statistics (all the columns to the right of the "Coefficients" column. These topics are not covered in this book.). In the "Coefficients" column, the intercept is shown as 3.97 (rounded to two decimal points) and the slope as 0.63 (shown as the coefficient for "employee number," the X variable in this example, because the slope b is the coefficient for X variable). So our regression equation is $Y = 3.97 + 0.63X$.

SUMMARY OUTPUT

Regression Statistics	
Multiple R	0.86011603
R Square	0.73979958
Adjusted R Square	0.73236528
Standard Error	6.43242463
Observations	37

ANOVA

	df	SS	MS	F	Significance F
Regression	1	4117.404538	4117.4	99.5117	9.03852E-12
Residual	35	1448.16303	41.376		
Total	36	5565.567568			

	Coefficients	Standard Error	t Stat	P-value	Lower 95%	Upper 95%
Intercept	3.96990478	1.451744341	2.7346	0.00974	1.022703486	6.9171061
employee number	0.62647359	0.062800876	9.9756	9E-12	0.498980876	0.7539663

Figure 8-7 Regression Result of Staff PCs and Employee Number

If we translate X and Y into the actual variables in this example, then the relationship between the two variables can be expressed as:

Staff PCs = 3.97+0.63×(number of employees).

Once we have the regression equation, we can use it to draw a regression line on the scatter plot. All we have to do is to pick two X values (choose two X values that are far apart to get a more accurate line) and plug them into the equation to calculate the corresponding Y values. We then locate these two data points on the scatter plot and link them to obtain the regression line. I have done this for the example we are working with and the result is shown in Figure 8-8.

The regression line on the scatter plot provides us with a visual impression of how well (or how poorly) the regression line "represents" the data points. The line in Figure 8-8 fits the data points fairly well but it would fit better if the line were turned counterclockwise a little. The cause for this imperfect "representation" is that one data point on the far right does not fit the general "upward trend" of other data points. Relative to its number of employees, this library has very

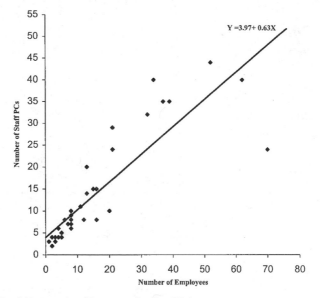

Figure 8-8   A Regression Line on a Scatter Plot

few staff PCs. This data point is called an "outlier." This particular outlier is also an influential data point because it has more influence on the regression equation and the regression line than "normal" data points. If we delete this data point and redo the regression analysis, the resulting regression equation and regression line would be quite different. When we encounter this kind of unusual data point in real data analysis, we should check to see if it is the result of an error in data collection or data input. If so, we should correct the mistake and redo the regression analysis, which will result in a regression line that better represents the data.

In Figure 8-8, the data points above the regression line and the data points below the line represent two different types of libraries in terms of number of staff PCs. Compared to their counterparts below the line, those libraries that are above the line have more staff PCs relative to the number of employees they have. Drawing the regression line on the scatter plot also allows us to examine what data points lie above the line or below the line to see if there is any pattern. If all or most of those libraries above the line are level A government libraries and those below the line are level B government libraries, then it may suggest that level A government libraries are better equipped with PCs.

8.7 Prediction

As explained earlier, we can predict one variable (usually the Y variable) based on the other (usually the X variable) once the regression equation is established. This can be done easily by plugging the X value into the equation and calculate the corresponding Y value. For the example we are working with, imagine that we are planning to open a new library and we want to know how many staff PCs are needed given that there will be 25 employees there. Plugging $X = 25$ into the regression equation $Y = 3.97 + 0.63X$, we get $Y = 20$; i.e., about 20 staff PCs will be needed if this new library is going to be comparable to other libraries in the number of staff PCs. Looking at Figure 8-8, we see that this data point ($X = 25$, $Y = 20$) falls exactly on the regression line, which is what should happen if the calculation is correct.

Like any other kind of prediction, a prediction based on a regression equation has the issue of accuracy. As data points are scattered around the regression line, there is a range of possible Y values associated with a given X value. The Y value predicted by the regression equation can be viewed as the "most probable" value for the given X value. The word "most probable" has a statistical meaning here. Remember that the data we collected and used to develop the regression equation are a random sample of the population data. If we take a different sample and estimate the regression coefficients a and b again, they may be slightly different from what we obtained from the first sample. We never know the true coefficient values of a and b in the population. What we can do is to give the best estimate based on the sample data we have and acknowledge that our prediction is not 100 percent accurate. Furthermore, we can have some idea of how accurate our prediction is. One way of doing so is to calculate the 95 percent confidence interval for our prediction. We will not get into the technical details of this calculation here. Interested readers can refer to other statistics books such as Howell (1997, 245–249).

Another way of knowing the accuracy of the prediction is through the coefficient of determination. The coefficient of determination is denoted by r^2 and calculated as the square of the correlation coefficient r. For the example data we are working with, r = 0.86, so the coefficient of determination is 0.86^2, which equals 0.74 (see the second line in the first part of the Excel output in Figure 8-7). Multiplying r^2 by 100, we get the percent of information about Y that is contained in X. In other words the coefficient of determination tells us the proportion of variability in Y that can be attributed to, or explained by, the variability in X. In general, the larger the coefficient of determination, the more useful X is in predicting Y and the more accurate the prediction will be. For our example data, we can say that 74 percent of the variability in the number of staff PCs among different libraries can be explained by the variability in the number of employees these libraries have. The remaining 26 percent of the variability can be attributed to other factors such as the level of funding the library receives.

The term coefficient of determination may sound new to you but the chances are that you have encountered it before in daily life. We often hear reports of research findings showing what factors contributed to a certain disease. For example, we may hear that diet contributed 20 percent to heart attacks and genetic factors 10 percent (note that the figures here are arbitrarily made up). People sometimes misunderstand the results of correlation analyses. For example, I once heard somebody saying that drunk driving caused 40 percent of the traffic accidents according to statistics, so sober drivers caused 60 percent of the accidents. Obviously, this interpretation does not make sense. How can sober driving be more dangerous than drunk driving! The statistics here are not comparing drunk driving vs. sober driving, but drunk driving vs. many other factors, including road condition, vehicle condition, unknown factors, etc., each of which contributed to the 60 percent not attributed to drunk driving.

In the regression analysis we are discussing in this chapter, there is only one independent variable X. In other words, we are explaining or predicting Y based on only one variable. In real life, there are often multiple factors or independent variables that contribute to or determine the dependent variable Y. In multiple regression, which will be discussed briefly in Chapter 13, we use several independent variables, X_1, X_2, etc., to predict or explain the dependent variable. Each independent variable contributes a portion to explaining or predicting the Y variable. If we can include all the X variables that contribute to Y, then the total coefficient of determination would be 1. Of course, this is hardly possible given that it is almost impossible to exhaust or include all the variables in a regression analysis.

8.8 Requirements for Doing Correlation and Regression

The following requirements must be met before a correlation and regression analysis can be carried out:

- The sample is unbiased and representative of the population. This requirement applies to any inferential statistical test as discussed in Chapter 6.
- Both variables are measured in interval or ratio scales, i.e., data are of interval or ratio type. To examine the relationship between two variables measured in nominal or ordinal scale, use the chi-square test discussed in Chapter 7.
- The two variables being studied are normally distributed. Significant departures from normality (e.g., badly skewed) will require use of the Spearman correlation coefficient test that will be discussed in Chapter 11.
- The relationship between the two variables is linear; i.e., the scatter plot shows a straight line pattern rather than a curve pattern. There are regression techniques covered in advanced statistics books that can deal with curve type relationships.

These are the requirements for the basic correlation and regression analysis covered in this book. There are other requirements that apply to other regression techniques such as estimating confidence intervals. See Howell (1997, 252–253, 265–268) for a detailed discussion.

CHAPTER 9

Are Two Samples Significantly Different? —T Test

When I introduced hypothesis testing in Section 5.9 of Chapter 5, I demonstrated the concept by testing the hypothesis that journalism students spend an average of six hours per week in the university library. In that hypothetical study, we sampled 50 journalism students and collected data on the hours they spend in the library. We then did a t test. On the basis of that t test result, we can either reject or fail to reject the null hypothesis of six hours per week. In this case, we are dealing with only one population (the journalism students) and we only have one sample (the 50 students sampled from the whole journalism student population), so it is called a one-sample t test.

More often, however, we will want to compare two populations and need to take a sample from each population, giving us two samples in total. For instance, we may want to compare journalism students to psychology students to see if the average hours spent in the library by the two student populations are the same or different. It would be too expensive to collect data from every student in both groups to obtain the population data. Instead, we will use inferential statistics to reach a conclusion about the populations based on two samples, one from each student population. We will calculate the average hours (the mean) for each sample, then use a t test to determine whether or not the difference between the two sample means is statistically significant. In other words, whether there is a real difference in the population means.

Before we proceed to carry out the t test, whether we do it manually or use software, we first have to decide which type of t test to use. There are two types of t test that are used to compare two means. One is called the independent-sample t test (independent t test for short) and the other is called the paired-sample t test (paired t test for short). These two types of t test, and when to use each one, are discussed in the next section.

9.1 Independent T Test vs. Paired T Test

Suppose we wanted to compare two different user interfaces for a new information retrieval system to see which one takes less time for users to learn and navigate. We decided to conduct an experiment to test these two interfaces using 80 users randomly selected from a user population of 1,000 people. Forty of these users were assigned to conduct a search using interface A. The other 40 users did a search with interface B. We recorded the time (in minutes) that it took for each user to perform the search task. After the experiment, we have two groups of data like the following:

	Interface A	Interface B
Time	14	25
	21	18
	22	22
	.	.
	.	.
	.	.

The means of groups A and B are calculated at 19 and 21 respectively. We must now determine whether the difference of two minutes between these two means is statistically significant. In other words, does interface A really take less time for the population (1,000 users) to learn and navigate or does it just happen to be so for the sample users (e.g., it happened that the samples included a few more users whose search habits fit interface A better)? To answer this question, we chose to do an independent t test because the two samples of data are independent of each other. In other words, the users are unrelated and were tested independently. Another way of looking at this issue is that the two numbers in each row of the sample data displayed above are not related at all. Rather, each number represents a different user.

An alternative design for this experiment is to select only 40 users, rather than 80. Each user would then conduct a search with each interface. To avoid the possible bias caused by the first interface searched, 20 users will search with interface A first and the other 20 users will search with interface B first. Recording the time each user spends using each interface, you will still get 80 numbers as in the first design.

	Interface A	Interface B
Time	14	20
	21	30
	22	33
	.	.
	.	.
	.	.

However, the two numbers in each row are now related. They are the results from the same user. These two figures will both be high for a novice user who generally takes more time to do any search. On the other hand, they will both be low for an expert searcher who will likely be faster with either interface. Once we calculate the means for the two groups of data, we will still face the same question: Is the difference in the means statistically significant or not? This time we will use a paired t test to find the answer because the data in each row are paired up.

We can now return to the example introduced earlier about comparing journalism students with psychology students on the average hours spent in the library. It is obvious that an independent t test should be used in this case because the two groups of collected data will be unrelated. On the other hand, if we want to determine whether a particular group of students, say the journalism students, spends more time in the university library or on the Internet, we can do either an independent t test or a paired t test depending on how the data will be collected. If we take a sample of 30 students and ask each to report both hours in the library and hours on the Internet, then we will do a paired t test. On the other hand, if we sample 60 students and ask 30 of them to report hours in the library and the other 30 to report hours on the Internet, then we will do an independent t test.

In some situations, such as the case of comparing journalism students to psychology students on the hours spent in the library, we have no choice but to design an independent t test. On other occasions, such as the information retrieval experiment discussed above, we can design either an independent t test or a paired t test. Which of the two designs is better and should thus be used? The paired t test design is better. The most obvious advantage for the paired design is that it needs fewer subjects, making it less expensive to collect data (it takes time and energy to recruit subjects, explain the study to them, etc.). A more important, although less obvious, advantage of the paired design is that the paired t test is a more powerful statistical test than the independent t test if the pairs of data are related. In statistical terms, "power" means the probability of finding a significant difference if there is one. So a paired t test, since it is the more powerful one, is more likely to reveal the difference between the two interfaces if they are truly different while an independent t test may fail to reveal the difference, especially when the difference is small. The reason that the paired t test is more powerful is that the paired design eliminates the individual differences among users (the two numbers on the same row are from the same person), thereby reducing the variability of the data. The test statistic, the t score, is inversely related to the variability, a topic that will be discussed in the next section.

9.2   The Logic of the T Test

The logic of the t test, whether independent or paired, is to decide whether there is a difference in the populations based on data from samples of those populations. Two factors are considered in this decision, sample mean difference and sample data variability.

Sample mean difference is the difference between the two sample means. Even if there is no difference in the population means, there could still be a small difference in the sample means due to randomness of the sampling (we happened to include a few more high scores or low scores from one of the two populations). However, the chance of having a large sample mean difference is not great if there is no population mean difference. So the larger the sample mean difference, the more likely it is that there is a difference in the populations.

We also consider the variability of the data. Given the same sample size and the same sample mean difference, greater variability makes it less likely that the sample mean difference is the result of a real population difference. To explain this point, let us look at the following two groups of data and suppose that the two groups are two populations (in reality, no population is so small, but for the sake of discussion we will only have six data points in each population):

Group A: 1, 2, 4, 8, 15, 30   Group B: 3, 5, 9, 10, 11, 22

Both groups of data have a mean of 10 (i.e., the population means are the same). Now we take a sample of three data points from each group and calculate the sample means. If we take the 2nd, 3rd, and 4th data points, the sample means will be 4.7 for Group A and 8.0 for Group B. The sample mean difference of 3.3 is not statistically significant because there is no mean difference in the populations. The reason we get this fairly large mean difference (relative to the means themselves) is because of the large variability in the two populations.

Now let us look at two other groups of data in which the variability is smaller:

Group C: 9, 9, 10, 10, 11, 11   Group D: 8, 9, 10, 11, 11, 12

The population means are still 10. We will still take a sample of three data points (still from the 2nd to the 4th data points) from each group. The sample means are 9.7 and 10 for Group C and Group D respectively. The mean difference is 0.3, much smaller than that for Group A and Group B.

You can repeat the above exercise many times by taking different samples from the populations. Overall, you will find that the sample mean differences for Groups A and B are greater than those for Groups C and D. The mean difference will also vary more from sample to sample for Groups A and B. This means that when the variability in the population is large, we are more likely to get a large sample mean difference even if there is no difference in the population means. Therefore, we have to take population variability into consideration in a t test. The greater the population variability, the more "reluctant" we should be to conclude that there is a population difference. This factor is reflected in the denominator of the t score, the test statistic for the t test, which is defined as:

$$t = \frac{\overline{X}_1 - \overline{X}_2}{SE_D}$$

In the t score formula, $\overline{x}_1$ and $\overline{x}_2$ are the means of sample 1 and sample 2 respectively. SE_D stands for the estimated standard error of the difference and is calculated based on sample variability (we never know the population variability so we use sample variability as an estimate of the population variability). There are various formulae to calculate SE_D for various situations, such as whether the t test being performed is independent or paired. We will not get into the details of this calculation because they may cause confusion and divert us from grasping the meaning of the t test. Instead, we will let computer software take care of formulae and calculations. What we do need to know is that SE_D reflects the variability issue discussed above. A larger SE_D means larger variability, which makes us less inclined to conclude a significant difference. Because the t score gets smaller as the SE_D grows larger, a smaller t score is associated with a lower probability of a significant difference. Or, to word it differently, the larger the t score the more likely it is that there is a difference in the population.

The numerator of the t score is the sample mean difference. The larger the sample mean difference, the larger the absolute value of the t score, and the more likely it is that there is a significant difference (the t score can be either positive or negative depending on which group of data is labeled as Group 1. Obviously, it is the absolute value of the t score, not its sign, which indicates the likelihood of a significant difference.). How large does the t score have to be for us to conclude a significant difference in the population means? We use a statistical table called Critical Values of t (t table for short), which is found in Appendix 5 of this book, to answer this question. The "critical value" is the value of the test statistic at which the p-value is at a pre-set level. If the absolute value of our calculated t score is equal to or greater than the critical t value, then the p-value is equal to or less than the pre-set level (usually 0.05) and we will conclude that the difference is statistically significant.

9.3   The Procedure of the T Test

The procedure for the t test, be it independent or paired, follows the general procedure for hypothesis testing that was outlined in Section 5.9 of Chapter 5. First, set up two competing hypotheses (Step 1). The null hypothesis assumes that there is no difference between the two population means and the alternative hypothesis states that the two means are different.[1] Next, calculate the test statistic, which is the t score (Step 2). The t score formula for an independent t test is different from that for a paired t test but we do not have to worry about this if we use software to do the calculation. We just have to specify the type of t test correctly. Then, determine the probability that the null hypothesis is true (the p-value) based on the t score by using the t table (Step 3). Finally, compare the p-value to the pre-set significance level, usually 0.05 (Step 4). If the p-value is equal to or less than the pre-set level, we will reject the null hypothesis and conclude that there is real difference in the population means. If the p-value is greater than the pre-set level, we will fail to reject the null hypothesis, which means that we have insufficient evidence to say that the two population means are different.

What is left to be explained is how to locate a critical value in the t table (Appendix 5). The first column of Appendix 5, labeled df, is the degrees of freedom. The calculation of df is different for different types of t tests, as I will discuss later. The second and third columns list the critical values for significance levels of 0.05 and 0.01 respectively. We usually use the 0.05 level, so that we will reject the null hypothesis when the probability for it to be true is equal to or less than 0.05. So, if df is calculated at 10, then the corresponding critical value is 2.228 for the significance level of 0.05. If the df you have calculated is not listed in the table, then you can either use the next smaller df that is listed or extrapolate from the two nearest df figures. For example, if your df is 37 and you want to use significance level of 0.05, the critical value can either be 2.028 (the one listed for df = 36) or 2.026 (the average of 2.028 for df = 36 and 2.024 for df = 38). As you can see, these two possible critical values are very close anyway, which is why there is no need to list all the possible df when it is greater than 30.

Degrees of freedom for the independent t test are calculated as N_1+N_2 -2, where N_1 is sample size 1 (the number of data points in sample 1) and N_2 is sample size 2. For the paired t test, df is calculated as N-1 where N is the number of pairs of data. In the example in Section 1 of this chapter, we tested two different user interfaces of an information retrieval system. If we selected 80 subjects and had each subject search with one of the two interfaces, we would then use the independent t test to analyze the data. The degrees of freedom would be 78 ($N_1 = 40$, $N_2 = 40$). If we selected 40 subjects and had each subject search in both interfaces, then we would do a paired t test to analyze the data. The degrees of freedom would be 39 (there will be 40 pairs of data). In both scenarios, we have 80 numbers recorded from the experiment but the df of the paired t test is half of that of the independent t test and the critical value will be different as a result.

The smaller df in the paired t test is understandable when you consider the nature of data in the two types of t tests. In the independent t test, data points are not related at all so the value of one data point does not restrict the value of any other data point. The only restriction for the 80 data points is the two sample means. Once you have decided the values of 78 data points, the values of the two remaining data points are not "free" to change because there is only one possible value for each remaining data point that fits the sample mean. Hence there are 78 degrees of freedom. For the paired t test, half of the data are related to the other half by "pairing." Because only half of the data are "free" to change, the degrees of freedom are reduced by 50 percent compared to the independent t test. For a given type of t test and a given significance level, the critical value increases as df decreases (see the t table in Appendix 5). This means that for a smaller size of sample, which has a smaller df, there is a higher standard to reject the null hypothesis and conclude a significant difference (the t score has to be higher in order to exceed the critical value). This is the way it should be because we should be less confident (more reluctant) to reach a conclusion from a smaller size of sample.

9.4   Examples of T Tests Using Software

For a demonstration of how to use software to do t tests, I will keep working on the hypothetical example introduced earlier about comparing two different user interfaces for an information retrieval system. In the first scenario, there are 80 subjects participating in the experiment. Forty of them did a search using interface A and the other 40 used interface B. The time it took (measured in minutes) for each subject to complete the search was recorded. We have decided that an independent t test should be used to compare the two groups of data. The null hypothesis of this t test is that there is no difference between interface A and interface B in the average amount of time users will take to carry out a search. It should be noted that the word "users" in the preceding sentence refers to the general user population, not just the 80 test subjects. The purpose of the test is to use the sample to find out about the population. The alternative hypothesis is that the time will be different; i.e., it will take less time to use one interface than the other. To demonstrate how to do an independent t test using software, I made up 80 hypothetical data points and entered them into SPSS. I then chose the menu options "Analyze," "Compare Means," "Independent-Samples T Test," and specified the variables. The SPSS output is shown in Figure 9-1 (part of the original output that deals with an advanced issue of the t test is omitted due to space limitations).

Group Statistics

	Interface	N	Mean	Std. Deviation	Std. Error Mean
Time	Interface A	40	19.03	6.97	1.10
	Interface B	40	21.39	5.50	.87

Independent Samples Test

		t test for Equality of Means						
							95% Confidence Interval of the Difference	
		t	df	Sig. (2-tailed)	Mean Difference	Std. Error Difference	Lower	Upper
Time	Equal variances assumed	-1.683	78	.096	-2.36	1.40	-5.16	.43
	Equal variances not assumed	-1.683	74	.097	-2.36	1.40	-5.16	.43

Figure 9-1 SPSS Output of an Independent T Test

Figure 9-1 consists of two tables. The first table displays the descriptive statistics of the two samples. Subjects searching with interface A took an average of 19.03 minutes to complete the search while those using interface B took an average of 21.39 minutes. Is this sample mean difference of 2.36 minutes statistically significant? In other words, will it really take less time for the user population to use interface A or did it just happen to be so in the sample? The t test result listed in the second table will provide the answer.

There are two sets of results in the second table; one for "equal variances assumed" and one for "equal variances not assumed." If the variabilities of the two samples are similar, then you look at the "equal variances assumed" scenario (sample standard deviations listed in the first table of the SPSS output indicate the variability). On the other hand, if the variabilities of the two samples are quite different, then you look at the "equal variances not assumed" scenario. The formulae to calculate the t score and other numbers are slightly different for these two different scenarios. However, the two sets of results are very close in most situations anyway so that it is not an issue as to which set of results to use. For the particular data we are working with, the variabilities of the two samples are close enough so that we can look at the "equal variances assumed" scenario.

The t score is calculated at -1.68 (listed under the heading "t"). We do not have to check the t table to find out the critical value for this t test, as discussed when we outlined the procedure for the test, because SPSS provides the p-value (listed under the heading "Sig. (2-tailed)"). Since the p-value of 0.096 is greater than 0.05, we fail to reject the null hypothesis. The difference of about two minutes in the samples is not statistically significant and could be the result of randomness; i.e., the samples may happen to include a few more people whose search style fit interface A better. For the general user population, the two interfaces may not be different on average.

The last two columns of the second table of Figure 9-1 show the 95 percent confidence interval of the difference. The lower and the upper limits of the confidence interval are -5.16 and 0.43 respectively. The meaning of these two numbers can be interpreted as follows. We know that the sample mean difference is -2.36 (interface A minus interface B) but we do not know the population mean difference. However, there is a 95 percent chance that the population mean difference will be somewhere between -5.16 and 0.43. The confidence interval includes zero, which means that there could be no difference. This echoes the t test conclusion that there is no significant difference. It is not surprising that the results of the confidence interval and the t test (a hypothesis test) agree because, as discussed in Chapter 5, confidence intervals and hypothesis testing can be viewed as two sides of the same coin.

Paired Samples Statistics

		Mean	N	Std. Deviation	Std. Error Mean
Pair 1	Interface A	19.06	40	6.76	1.07
	Interface B	22.33	40	7.41	1.17

Paired Samples Correlations

		N	Correlation	Sig.
Pair 1	Interface A & Interface B	40	.586	.000

Paired Samples Test

		Paired Differences							
					95% Confidence Interval of the Difference				
		Mean	Std. Deviation	Std. Error Mean	Lower	Upper	t	df	Sig (2-tailed)
Pair 1	Interface A - Interface B	-3.27	6.48	1.02	-5.34	-1.20	-3.195	39	.003

Figure 9-2 SPSS Output of a Paired T Test

For an example of a paired t test, let us consider the second scenario of the information retrieval experiment where 40, rather than

80, subjects were recruited into the study. Each subject did a search with each interface. The time they took to complete each search was recorded. The null and alternative hypotheses for this t test are the same as those for the independent t test stated in the previous example. Again, I made up hypothetical data and entered them into SPSS. The menu options to go through for a paired t test in SPSS are "Analyze," "Compare Means," and "Paired-Samples T Test." The output is as shown in Figure 9-2.

The first table of Figure 9-2 lists descriptive statistics, such as means and standard deviations, for the two samples. The second table shows the correlation between the two samples. SPSS output includes this correlation coefficient test so that we can use it to confirm that the data are indeed related. Given that each pair of data points is from the same searcher, it is not surprising that the correlation coefficient test, as discussed in Chapter 8, shows that the correlation is statistically significant (p-value is listed under "Sig." as ".000," less than 0.05).

The result of the paired t test is summarized in the third table of Figure 9-2. The sample mean difference is -3.27 (interface A minus interface B). The t score is -3.195. Again, we do not have to use the t table because the p-value is provided in the output. Since the p-value of 0.003 is less than 0.05, we reject the null hypothesis and accept the alternative hypothesis. The sample mean difference of -3.27 is statistically significant. We can expect that the user population will take less time to search with interface A than with interface B. Although we know that the subjects in the sample took an average of about three more minutes to search with interface B, we do not know exactly what the time difference will be for the general user population. However, we can be 95 percent sure that it will be between 1.2 and 5.34 minutes. (See the numbers listed under the heading "95 percent confidence interval of the difference." Because the difference is calculated as interface A minus interface B and the latter takes more time, there are negative signs in front of the numbers.) This confidence interval does not include zero (the point of no difference), meaning that there is a difference between the two interfaces. Again, the results from hypothesis testing and confidence interval echo each other.

9.5 Requirements for Using a T Test

Both the independent t test and the paired t test have underlying assumptions about the data, therefore the data must meet the following requirements before a t test can be carried out (Diekhoff, 1996, 203, Sprinthall, 1997, 199):
- The samples are randomly selected.
- The sample data are of interval or ratio type.
- The two populations are approximately normally distributed.
- The standard deviations of the two samples must be fairly similar.

The first requirement, which means that the samples must be unbiased, applies to any inferential statistical test as discussed in Chapter 6. It does not rule out the use of stratified or systematic samples as long as they are unbiased. A biased sample will lead to a biased conclusion no matter what test is used. The second requirement is easy to understand. If the two groups of data being compared are of ordinal type, we should use a nonparametric test. (See Chapter 11 for a detailed discussion of nonparametric tests.) We do not usually know for sure if the third requirement, also called the normality requirement, is met because we do not have population data. However, the frequency distributions of the sample data will give us some idea of how the populations are distributed. If the sample distributions are badly skewed, then the requirement is not met. The fourth requirement, the homogeneity of variance requirement, is more restrictive for an independent t test if the sizes of the two samples are unequal (Howell, 1997, 201). In other words, not meeting the requirement will have less of a consequence if sample sizes are equal. Therefore, it is better to make the two sample sizes equal whenever possible. When requirements 3 and 4 are not met we can use nonparametric tests, to be discussed in Chapter 11, to test the hypothesis of difference. In addition to the above four requirements, the independent t test also requires that the two samples be truly independent of each other.

Endnote

1. This alternative hypothesis is "two-tailed," which means that it does not specify the direction of difference (whether the mean of population A is greater than the mean of population B or the other way around). There is also the "one-tailed" t test in which the direction of the difference is specified in the alternative hypothesis. The "one-tailed" t test requires a t table different from that of the "two-tailed" t test. The "one-tailed" t test is controversial and not very common so we will omit it in this book. Interested readers can refer to other statistics books such as Sprinthall (1997, 195–198).

CHAPTER 10

Are Three or More Samples Significantly Different?— Analysis of Variance

Analysis of variance, ANOVA for short, is an inferential statistical test used to determine if the differences among three or more sample means are statistically significant. That is, we use it to see if there are differences among the corresponding population means. There are numerous situations in information science in which we want to compare three or more means (averages) and can therefore use ANOVA. Imagine that you want to compare the quality of research conducted by faculty members in three different information science faculties and you use the citation rate (number of times a faculty member's papers are cited by other authors) as one of the measures. Rather than collecting citation data for hundreds of papers published by all the faculty members involved (the population data), you can take random samples of papers from each faculty and collect citation data for these sample papers. You can then conduct an analysis of variance test on the sample data to determine if the average citation rates for the three faculties (the populations) are the same or different. Another example would be a study to compare funding levels of information centers in four different states. You could collect funding data from a random sample of, say, 25 information centers from each state, calculate the average funding amount for each of the four samples and then use ANOVA to determine if the sample differences are statistically significant.

If you have read Chapter 9 in which the t test was discussed, you know that the t test can be used to compare two sample means to see whether or not they are significantly different. This may lead you to think that we can use multiple t tests, rather than ANOVA, to determine if three or more sample means are significantly different. For example, to determine if three samples labeled A, B, and C are significantly different, we can do three t tests. First, we compare A vs. B, then B vs. C, and finally A vs. C. Why do we introduce a new test when the familiar t test can do the job? What is the advantage of a single ANOVA over the multiple t tests? The obvious advantage is that it saves time and energy to do one ANOVA instead of several t tests. When the number of groups being compared increases beyond three, the number of possible comparisons and therefore the number of t tests increases dramatically.

An even more important advantage of ANOVA concerns the type I error rate. As discussed in Section 5.10 of Chapter 5, type I error occurs when we reject a null hypothesis that is actually correct. If we set our significance level at 0.05, then the chance of a type I error is 5 percent every time we reject a null hypothesis. When we reject null hypotheses again and again in multiple t tests, the type I error will multiply, sometimes to a dangerously high level.[1] Therefore, the type I error rate in multiple t tests can be much higher than in a single ANOVA, where it remains at the 0.05 level. For this reason, we should always use ANOVA instead of multiple t tests when comparing three or more groups.

10.1   The Logic of ANOVA

Perhaps the most interesting aspect of ANOVA is how it uses variance, a measure of variability, to examine the difference between means, a measure of central tendency. In other words, ANOVA determines whether the mean difference is statistically significant by analyzing the variance (hence the term "analysis of variance"). To understand how this works, we first need to explain the two types of variability that ANOVA examines.

The first type is called between group variability and measures how much the sample means vary from each other. The larger the mean differences, the larger the between group variability. It is easy to understand how this type of variability affects the determination of a significant difference. Logically, if the means of the samples are far apart then they are more likely to be significantly different. For instance, we would be more likely to conclude a significant difference if the means were 1, 20, and 30 than if they were 1, 1.2, and 1.3. Therefore, we can establish the principle that **the larger the between group variability, the more likely it is that there is a significant difference**.

The second type of variability is called within group variability, and it measures the variability of the data within each group. To see how this variability affects the determination of the significance of the difference, let us look at a hypothetical example. Suppose that you are comparing the citation rates of papers from three different information science faculties (the example introduced at the beginning of this chapter). You select five papers (this unusually small sample size is used for the convenience of discussion) from each faculty and collect their citation rates. Tables 10-1 and 10-2 present two hypothetical scenarios of data collection results.

Table 10-1   Significant Difference (Small Within Group Variability)

Faculty A	Faculty B	Faculty C
4	7	10
3	8	9
2	6	9
5	7	11
2	8	11
Mean = 3.2 Standard deviation = 1.3	Mean = 7.2 Standard deviation = 0.84	Mean = 10 Standard deviation = 1

Table 10-2   No Significant Difference (Large Within Group Variability)

Faculty A	Faculty B	Faculty C
2	3	3
4	11	6
2	7	9
10	6	11
3	9	15
Mean = 4.2 Standard deviation = 3.3	Mean = 7.2 Standard deviation = 3	Mean = 8.8 Standard deviation = 4.6

The mean differences in each scenario are similar, therefore, the between group variability is similar. However, by comparing the standard deviations of the groups in the two tables, we can see that the data in Table 10-1 have a lower variability within each group. A graphical representation of the data in each table will make the contrast between the two scenarios clearer. Assuming that the citation rates have a normal distribution, then the data in Table 10-1 and Table 10-2 can be represented by Figure 10-1 and Figure 10-2 respectively.

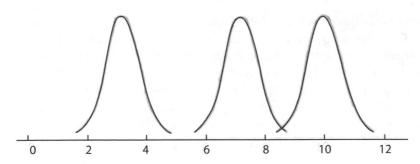

Figure 10-1   Graphical Representation of Data in Table 10-1

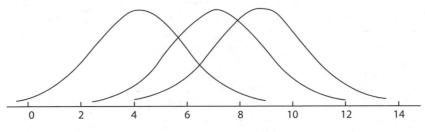

Figure 10-2   Graphical Representation of Data in Table 10-2

We can see that the means are spaced out in a similar fashion in both figures. However, the lower within group variability in Figure 10-1 means that the curves of the three samples do not spread out very far from their means. Because of this, they appear as three distinct and unrelated curves. In contrast, the higher within group variability in Figure 10-2 causes the curves of the three samples to spread out to the point where they overlap heavily in spite of the distance between their means. Indeed, each group in Figure 10-2 includes the means of its neighbors. If you were asked to choose which of the two scenarios represents a significant mean difference, you would pick Figure 10-1 because the samples in Figure 10-1 are distinct from each other, whereas there is less of a distinction for samples in Figure 10-2.

We now have two principles for determining significance of the mean difference using variability. First, **the larger the between group variability, the more likely it is that there is a significant difference**. Second, **the smaller the within group variability, the more likely it is that there is a significant difference**. The ANOVA test statistic, the F score, incorporates both of these principles by calculating the ratio of these two types of variability.

F = (between group variability) / (within group variability)

Calculated in this way, the F score will increase when between group variability increases and decrease when within group variability increases. If we apply the two principles discussed above, this means that a higher F score increases the likelihood that there is a significant difference among the means. Because of this, F score is used as the test statistic to decide whether or not to reject the null hypothesis of no difference. The F score is named for the British statistician R.A. Fisher who developed this statistical test. ANOVA is also called the F test for the same reason.

The actual mathematical formula for the F score looks rather complicated, but we do not have to deal with it. It is not likely that anybody today would calculate the F score manually rather than using software, so I will omit the formula here. All we need to know is that both the between group variability and within group variability are measured by variance (see Chapter 4 if you are interested in the details of calculating variance). It should be clear now why we can reach conclusions about mean differences by analyzing variability.

10.2 The Procedure for ANOVA

The procedure for the analysis of variance test reflects both its logic and the general procedure for hypothesis testing outlined in Section 5.9 of Chapter 5. First, we set up two competing hypotheses. The null hypothesis states that there is no difference among the population means under comparison; i.e., all the population means are equal. The alternative hypothesis states the opposite, that not all the population means are equal. In other words, at least one of the population means is different from the others. It should be pointed out that the alternative hypothesis encompasses all possible scenarios of difference: that only one group differs from the remaining groups that are equal to each other; that all the groups are different from each other; that there is some other pattern of differences.

Once we have formulated the hypotheses, the next step is to calculate the test statistic, the F score, which is usually done using computer software. The third step is to determine the probability that the null hypothesis is true (the p-value) based on the F score. I will explain how to do this in the next paragraph. The last step is to compare the p-value to the pre-set significance level, usually 0.05. If the p-value is greater than 0.05, we will fail to reject the null hypothesis, which means that we have insufficient evidence to prove that the population means under comparison are different from each other. On the other hand, if the p-value is equal to or less than the pre-set level, we will reject the null hypothesis and accept the alternative hypothesis. Because the alternative hypothesis does not specify the pattern of difference, we then need to further analyze the data to determine exactly how the population means differ. This can be accomplished by a further statistical test, which will be covered in Section 4 of this chapter. There is no sense in carrying out this extra test if the null hypothesis is not rejected, since the population means are all the same in this case and there is no pattern of difference to be further investigated.

How do we determine the probability that the null hypothesis is true, the p-value, based on the calculated F score? As was explained earlier in the chapter when discussing the logic of ANOVA, the larger the F score, the greater the probability that there is a difference in the population means and, therefore, the lower the probability that the null hypothesis is true. How large does the F score have to be so that the p-value will reach the pre-set value (usually 0.05) for us to reject the null hypothesis? The statistical table called Critical Values of F for ANOVA (F table for short) shown in Appendix 6 will answer this question. The "critical value" is the value of the test statistic at which the p-value is at a pre-set level. The statistical term "critical value" is similar to the term "threshold value" in our daily language. When the calculated F score is equal to or greater than the critical value, the p-value is equal to or less than the pre-set value so that we can reject the null hypothesis.

To locate a critical value in the F table, we need to know two degrees of freedom figures. One is called the between group degrees of freedom, symbolized as df_b, and the other is the within group degrees of freedom, symbolized as df_w.[2] The former is calculated as K-1, where K is the number of groups being compared. The latter is calculated as N-K, where N is the total number of data points of all the groups combined. Once you have these two figures, locating the critical value in the F table (Appendix 6) is very easy. Just look down the column corresponding to df_b until you reach the row corresponding to df_w. It should be noted that Appendix 6 is the F table for the significance level of 0.05. If you are using a different significance level, say 0.01, then you have to use a different F table. F tables for significance levels other than 0.05 are not included in this book because these levels are not commonly used.

For the example data in Table 10-1 or Table 10-2, K = 3 and N = 15. Using these figures, we can calculate that the between group degrees of freedom is 2 and the within group degrees of freedom is 12. Appendix 6 shows the critical value to be 3.885. For the data in Table 10-1, Excel calculated the F score to be 51.5. (The output is omitted here. I will show how to read the Excel output for ANOVA in the next section.) Because the calculated F score is greater than the critical value, we reject the null hypothesis of no difference and conclude that the three population means are not all the same. For data in Table 10-2, the F score is calculated at 1.97. Since this is less than the critical value, we fail to reject the null hypothesis; i.e., we failed to prove that the three population means are different. These two F test results confirm the conclusions we reached earlier by looking at the data and the graphs (Figure 10-1 and Figure 10-2). Data in these two tables are artificially made simple so that we can reach a conclusion by just looking at the data. Normally, we will not be able to do so without a statistical test, as the example in the next section will show.

10.3 Example of ANOVA Using Software

The data that I will analyze to demonstrate the complete process of doing ANOVA are taken from a survey carried out to study the use of various information sources for business purposes in the small business sector (Vaughan et al., 1996). The study was conducted in London, Ontario, so the population refers to all the small businesses in the area and the sample refers to the businesses participating in the study. One of the sources investigated was the public library and one of the questions asked was "What would be the impact on your business of closing the library?" (here "the library" refers to the local public library). Answers to the question were classified into four categories: no impact, minimal impact, some impact, and significant impact. In the survey, we also collected data on various business characteristics including business age (the number of years that the business had existed). It had been suggested that younger businesses have more need for library services than mature, well-established businesses. If this theory is correct, then the younger businesses will be more affected by the closing of the public library. In other words, businesses in the significant-impact group should be younger on average than those in the no-impact or minimal-impact groups. To find out if this is true, we can carry out an analysis of variance test to compare business ages of different impact groups.

The numbers of businesses in the four impact groups (from no impact to significant impact) are 61, 32, 9, and 32 respectively. Because ANOVA is more robust[3] when sample sizes are equal, I will make the sample sizes equal by omitting the some-impact group (only has 9 businesses) and taking a random sample of 32 from the 61 businesses in the no-impact group. As a result, there are three groups in ANOVA each with 32 businesses. The null hypothesis is that in the population the average business ages of the three impact groups are the same. In other words, businesses of different ages have the same need for the public library so that the closing of it will have the same level of impact on them. The alternative hypothesis is that the average business ages for the three impact groups are not all the same in the population.

Once the hypotheses are specified, the next step is to calculate the F score. Excel is used for this purpose. To do ANOVA in Excel, go through menu options "Tools," "Data Analysis," "Anova: Single Factor," and then specify input range (where the data are located) and output range (where the result should go). The Excel result is shown in Figure 10-3.

ANOVA: Single Factor

SUMMARY

Groups	Count	Sum	Average	Variance
no impact	32	629	19.66	723.85
minimal impact	32	361	11.28	138.27
significant impact	32	249	7.78	76.89

ANOVA

Source of Variation	SS	df	MS	F	P-value	F crit
Between Groups	2383	2	1191.50	3.81	0.03	3.09
Within Groups	29109.16	93	313.00			
Total	31492.16	95				

Figure 10-3   Excel Output of ANOVA

The Excel output consists of two parts. The first part, titled "Summary," presents descriptive statistics for the three groups under comparison. "Count" is the number of data points in each group. "Sum" and "Average" list the total age and the average age respectively. "Variance" is the square of standard deviation. For example, the variance for the no-impact group is 723.85, so its standard deviation is 26.9. The average ages for the three groups are calculated at 19.66, 11.28, and 7.78 respectively. Are these sample mean differences statistically significant (i.e., reflecting real differences in the population)? The ANOVA result presented in the second part of the Excel output will answer this question. The F score (listed under "F" in the Excel output) is calculated at 3.81, greater than the critical value of 3.09 (listed under "F crit"), so we will reject the null hypothesis and accept the alternative hypothesis. If the software package that you are using does not present the critical value, you can find it in the F table as was discussed in the previous section of this chapter. Excel also lists the p-value as 0.03, meaning that there is only a 3 percent chance that the null hypothesis is true. Our decision to reject the null hypothesis is confirmed here since the p-value is less than 0.05.

The alternative hypothesis that we accepted states that the average business ages for the three impact groups are not all the same in the population. However, we cannot tell from the ANOVA result whether one group differs from the other two or all three groups are different from each other. To know the pattern of difference, we need to analyze the data further.

10.4 Examining the Pattern of Difference

There are several statistical tests that can be used to examine the pattern of mean difference, e.g., the Scheffé test and the Student-Newman-Keuls test. However, the one most commonly introduced in basic statistics books is the Tukey's HSD test, short for Tukey's Honestly Significant Difference test. Some software, such as SPSS, will do this test for you while others, such as Excel, cannot. Therefore, it is necessary to discuss how to carry out this test manually. As you will see, it is a very straightforward test to do. I will keep using the example data that we have been working with to demonstrate how to carry out a Tukey's HSD test.

There are two steps in a Tukey's HSD test. First, we calculate the HSD score, which is defined as:

$$HSD = q\sqrt{\frac{MS_{within}}{n}}$$

where MS_{within} stands for within group mean square. It is the within group variability, the denominator of the F score, discussed earlier in this chapter. We do not have to calculate the value of MS_{within} manually because it is part of the ANOVA result (the second part of Figure 10-3). It is listed as 313, located at the intersection of row "Within Groups" and the column "MS." The "n" in the HSD formula is the number of data points in each group when sample sizes are equal. Equal sample size means each group has the same number of data points, as is the case for our example data. If the sample sizes are unequal, then we have to calculate the harmonic mean sample size (see Howell, 1997, 222, if interested). The value of "q" in the HSD formula can be found in Appendix 7, Critical Values for Tukey's HSD. To locate the value of q in Appendix 7, we need the following two figures: the number of groups and the within group degrees of freedom, df_w. Recall that df_w is calculated as N-K where N is the total number of data points of all the groups and K is the number of groups (see Section 10.2 of this chapter).

For our example data, there are 3 groups and 32 data points in each group. So df_w is 93 (96 data points minus 3 groups). The df_w is also shown in the ANOVA result in Figure 10-3 (intersection of column "df" and row "Within Groups"). Looking at Appendix 7, $df_w = 93$ is not listed and the two closest df_w figures are $df_w = 60$ and $df_w = 120$. When K = 3 (we have 3 groups), q is 3.4 for $df_w = 60$ and 3.36 for $df_w = 120$. We will simply use the average of these two q values, which is 3.38. Plugging n = 32, $MS_{within} = 313$, q = 3.38 into the HSD formula, we get:

$$HSD = q\sqrt{\frac{MS_{within}}{n}} = 3.38 \times \sqrt{\frac{313}{32}} = 3.38 \times 3.13 = 10.58$$

Once we have the HSD score, the next step is to calculate the difference between all the possible pairs of means and then compare each mean difference against the HSD score. If the mean difference is equal to or greater than the HSD score, we will conclude that the difference is statistically significant. This means that there is a real difference between the two groups in the population. On other hand, if the mean difference is less than the HSD score, we will say that the difference is not statistically significant, meaning that there is no difference between the two population means.

For our example data, the three means are 19.66 for the no-impact group, 11.28 for the minimal-impact group, and 7.78 for the significant-impact group. The results of the three possible pairs of mean comparisons are as follows:

— The mean difference between the no-impact and minimal-impact group is 8.38, less than the HSD score, so the difference is not statistically significant.

— The mean difference between the minimal-impact and significant-impact group is 3.5, also less than the HSD score, thus there is no real difference between these two groups in the population either.

— The mean difference between the no-impact and significant-impact group is 11.88, greater than the HSD score, so we can conclude that these two groups do differ in their population means.

Summarizing the ANOVA and HSD test results, we can say that the average business ages for the three groups under comparison are not all the same and the difference is between the no-impact group and the significant-impact group. The average business age for the no-impact group is 19.66 years, more than twice as old as the significant-impact group whose average business age is 7.78. This means that closing the public library will have more impact on young businesses than on old businesses. In other words, younger businesses have more need for library services than their mature, well-established counterparts. This is obviously useful information for public libraries in designing their services to the business community.

As mentioned earlier, SPSS has a Tukey's HSD test function built into it. For a comparison with our manual calculation result, I carried out the test for our example data in SPSS. It is not difficult for us to understand the computer output because we know how the test is done manually. Figure 10-4 is the SPSS output.

In the SPSS output, each mean difference appears twice, once as Group A minus Group B, and once as the reverse. As a result, there are six mean differences rather than three, half of which are negative. If we ignore the negative signs, the mean difference figures are the same as those that we calculated manually. SPSS marks significant mean differences by an asterisk (*). There is only one such mean difference, 11.8750, which is the difference between the no-impact group and the significant-impact group. So the SPSS result confirms our manual calculation result.

Multiple Comparisons

Dependent Variable: business age
Tukey HSD

(I) IMPACT	(J) IMPACT	Mean Difference (I-J)	Std. Error	Sig.	95% Confidence Interval	
					Lower Bound	Upper Bound
no impact	minimal impact	8.3750	4.4230	.146	-2.1597	18.9097
	significant impact	11.8750*	4.4230	.023	1.3403	22.4097
minimal impact	no impact	-8.3750	4.4230	.146	-18.9097	2.1597
	significant impact	3.5000	4.4230	.709	-7.0347	14.0347
significant impact	no impact	-11.8750*	4.4230	.023	-22.4097	-1.3403
	minimal impact	-3.5000	4.4230	.709	-14.0347	7.0347

*. The mean difference is significant at the .05 level.

Figure 10-4   A SPSS Output of Tukey's HSD Test

The SPSS output also shows the 95 percent confidence interval for each mean difference (the last two columns of Figure 10-4). What is the meaning of this confidence interval? It is an estimate of the population mean difference based on the sample mean difference. For example, the sample mean difference between the no-impact and minimal-impact groups is 8.38. We do not know exactly what the mean difference would be between these two groups in the population. However, based on the confidence interval figures, we can be 95 percent certain that it would be somewhere between -2.16 and 18.91 (see the first line of confidence interval figures in Figure 10-4, rounded to two decimal points). Note that this confidence interval ranges from negative to positive and therefore includes zero. This tells us that the difference in the population could be zero, meaning that there is no difference. Tukey's HSD test, a hypothesis test, reached the same conclusion that the difference between these two groups is not statistically significant. The confidence interval for the mean difference between the no-impact group and the significant-impact group is shown as 1.34 to 22.41 (second line in Figure 10-4). This confidence interval does not include zero, meaning that the mean difference in the population is not zero. Again, Tukey's HSD test reached the same conclusion.

10.5 Requirements for Using ANOVA

The following requirements must be met before ANOVA can be carried out (Sprinthall, 1997, 293):
- The sample groups are randomly and independently selected.
- The data are of interval or ratio type.
- There is a normal distribution in the population from which the sample is selected.
- The variability within groups should be fairly similar.

The requirement for random sampling is to guard against bias. It does not exclude the use of unbiased systematic or stratified samples. The independent selection of samples requires that data in different groups be independent of each other. If you have read about the t test in Chapter 9, you know that there are two types of t test, the independent t test and the paired t test. The two groups of data in the independent t test are independent of each other while the two groups of data in the paired t tests are related. ANOVA can be viewed as an extension of the independent t test in that the number of groups being compared are extended from two to three or more. If the three or more groups under comparison are related (a possible but rare situation), then we should use the repeated-measures ANOVA, a topic not covered in this book.

The second requirement is understandable because ANOVA tests the mean differences and the mean should be used only for interval and ratio data. The third and fourth requirements, called the normality requirement and the homogeneity of variance requirement respectively, are imposed because the analysis of variance test is based on the assumption that data are normally distributed and the groups under comparison have similar variability. However, ANOVA is a very robust statistical test, which means that not meeting the requirements will have relatively minor consequences. This is especially true for the normality requirement. It is important to note, however, that heterogeneity of variance and unequal sample sizes do not mix. If you have reason to anticipate unequal variances, make every effort to keep your sample sizes as equal as possible (Howell, 1997, 321). When data are of ordinal type (not meeting requirement 2) or the normality and homogeneity of variance requirements are seriously violated (not meeting requirements 3 and 4), we can consider using the Kruskal-Wallis test covered in the next chapter.

The ANOVA discussed in this chapter involves only one independent variable. Therefore, it is also called one-way ANOVA. In our example of evaluating citation rates for different faculties, the faculty is the sole independent variable (citation rate is the dependent variable). If we wanted to compare the citation rates based on two independent variables, e.g., faculty and whether or not the author was tenured, then we would have to resort to two-way ANOVA, a more advanced technique that will be discussed in Chapter 13.

Endnotes

1. The formula to calculate type I error in multiple t tests is $1-(1-\alpha)^n$, where n is the number of times null hypotheses are rejected and α is the significance level. So if $\alpha = 0.05$ and three t tests all rejected the null hypothesis, then type I error will be $1-(1-0.05)^3 = 0.14$.

2. Because the numerator of the F score is the between group variability and the denominator is the within group variability, between group degrees of freedom is also called degrees of freedom for numerator and the within group degrees of freedom is also called degrees of freedom for denominator. You may encounter this terminology in some other statistics books.

3. Robust means less sensitive to the violation of ANOVA requirements, which will be discussed in the last section of this chapter.

CHAPTER 11

When Data Do Not Behave— Using Nonparametric Tests

All the inferential statistical tests discussed so far have requirements that must be satisfied before the test can be conducted. The requirements for each test are discussed at the end of the chapter covering the test. All the tests have one requirement in common: The sample being tested is a random sample. The t test, ANOVA, and the Pearson correlation coefficient test also require that the variables under study be normally distributed (the normality requirement). The t test and ANOVA further have a homogeneity requirement that means that the groups being compared have similar variability, i.e., similar standard deviation. What if the sample is random (this is under our control), but the data do not behave? That is, they do not meet the normality and/or homogeneity requirements (this is not under our control). Do we have to abandon the data? No. We can resort to nonparametric tests.

The word nonparametric means that there are no requirements on parameters such as standard deviation. Nonparametric tests are also called distribution free tests because they do not require that the data be normally distributed. Although we have just introduced the concept of nonparametric test now, we have already learned a nonparametric test. The chi-square test discussed in Chapter 7 is a nonparametric test. If you check the requirements for the chi-square test, you will find that it does not have normality and homogeneity requirements. On the other hand, the Pearson correlation coefficient test, the t test, and ANOVA (Chapters 8–10) are all parametric tests because they do have one or both of these requirements. There are many nonparametric tests. In this chapter we will introduce those that can be used as alternatives when the requirements for the t test, ANOVA, and the Pearson Correlation coefficient test are not met. Microsoft Excel (all versions up to and including Excel 2000) cannot perform any of the nonparametric tests discussed in this chapter, so SPSS will be used to analyze the data in the examples for this chapter.

All nonparametric tests covered in this chapter follow the standard procedure for statistical tests outlined in Section 5.9 of Chapter 5. First, we formulate a null hypothesis and an alternate hypothesis. The null hypothesis is always that there is no relationship (or no difference) while the alternative is that the relationship (or difference) exists. Once we have the hypotheses, we calculate a test statistic from the data, then use the test statistic to determine the probability that the null hypothesis is true (the p-value). If the p-value is below a set level (usually 0.05), then we reject the null hypothesis and accept the alternative hypothesis.

11.1 Spearman Correlation Coefficient

As the nonparametric counterpart of the Pearson correlation coefficient, the Spearman Correlation coefficient can be used to determine whether two variables are related when the requirements for the Pearson correlation coefficient test are not met. In other words, the Spearman correlation coefficient can be used in the following situations:
- Both variables are measured in ordinal scale.
- One of the variables is measured in ordinal scale but the other one in interval or ratio scale.
- Both variables are measured in interval or ratio scale but the requirements of a Pearson correlation coefficient test are not met; e.g., the frequency distribution for one or both variables is badly skewed.

The Spearman correlation coefficient, also referred to as Spearman's rho, is symbolized by r_s, as opposed to r_p for the Pearson correlation coefficient. A formula is used to calculate r_s, which indicates the strength of the relationship between the two variables being studied.

To illustrate how we use r_s to test the hypothesis of a relationship, suppose that you are hired as a consultant by the Ontario Library Association to find out if public library circulation is related to the number of reference questions received. Rather than gathering data from all the libraries, you randomly select 32 libraries and collect their circulation and reference data.[1] You can then use inferential statistics to reach a conclusion about the population (all the public libraries in Ontario) based on the sample data. Your null hypothesis is that there is no relationship between circulation and reference and your alternative hypothesis is that the two variables are related (recall that even if you suspect a relationship, your null hypothesis should always be that there is no relationship, as discussed in Section 7.6 of Chapter 7). Because the circulation and reference figures are ratio data, your initial thought is to use the Pearson correlation coefficient. To check if the requirements of the Pearson correlation coefficient are met, you did a histogram for both variables and they look badly skewed as shown in Figure 11-1.

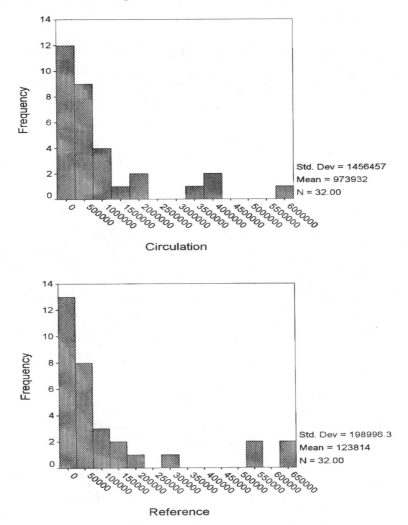

Figure 11-1 Frequency Distributions for Circulation and Reference Data

Apparently, the normality requirement of the Pearson correlation coefficient test is not met, so the Spearman correlation coefficient, r_s, should be used instead. Before calculating r_s, you need to convert the ratio data into ordinal data as r_s is calculated on ordinal data. We do this conversion by ranking the circulation and reference data. For the convenience of discussion, let us use data from only four libraries as shown in Table 11-1 to illustrate the process. The ranking results are shown to the right of the original data being ranked. Note that the original data are ranked from low to high here. You can also rank data from high to low since the direction of ranking will not affect the value of the Spearman correlation coefficient.

Table 11-1   Illustration of Ranking Data for Spearman Correlation Coefficient

Circulation	Circulation Ranking	Reference	Reference Ranking
200,000	1	3,000	1
300,000	3	4,000	2
250,000	2	6,000	4
500,000	4	5,000	3

The ranking data are ordinal data and the r_s is calculated on these data. The conversion is demonstrated here for the purpose of illustration only. If you input the original data into a software package such as SPSS, the software will do the conversion as part of the process of calculating r_s, so that normally you do not have to do the ranking manually. To perform a Spearman correlation coefficient test in SPSS, go through the menu options "Analyze," "Correlate," "Bivariate," and then specify variables and select "Spearman" in the popup screen. The SPSS output for the example data is shown in Figure 11-2.

Nonparametric Correlations

Correlations

			circulation	reference
Spearman's rho	circulation	Correlation Coefficient	1.000	.946**
		Sig. (2-tailed)	.	.000
		N	32	32
	reference	Correlation Coefficient	.946**	1.000
		Sig. (2-tailed)	.000	.
		N	32	32

**. Correlation is significant at the .01 level (2-tailed).

Figure 11-2   SPSS Output of a Spearman Correlation Coefficient Test

The Spearman correlation coefficient is shown to be 0.946. The possible value of a Spearman correlation coefficient ranges from -1 to +1, the same as the value of the Pearson correlation coefficient. Its meaning is also the same as that of the Pearson correlation coefficient: -1 means a perfect negative relationship between the two variables; +1 indicates a perfect positive relationship; and zero shows no relationship between the two variables. A greater absolute value for r_s makes it more likely that the relationship is statistically significant and therefore less likely that the null hypothesis, which assumes no relationship, is true. In other words, the greater the absolute value of r_s, the smaller the p-value. How large does r_s have to be for us to reject the null hypothesis and conclude a significant relationship? SPSS also shows the p-value for the test so we can determine the significance. In this case, the p-value is almost zero (shown as .000 in the line marked "Sig. (two-tailed)" in Figure 11-2). Because the p-value is far below our set value of 0.05, we can reject the null hypothesis and confidently say that a relationship between circulation and reference does exist in Ontario public libraries (the population), not just in the sample. Indeed, the r_s value of 0.946 indicates a very strong positive relationship between circulation and reference. The larger the circulation of a library, the more reference questions the library will receive and vice versa.

Although a very strong correlation is established here, no causation can be concluded. A large circulation may or may not cause a larger number of reference questions or vice versa. It is more likely that both variables are "caused" by a third variable, population served by the library. A larger population will result in both a larger circulation and a larger number of reference questions. As discussed in Section 8.5 of Chapter 8, correlation simply does not address the issue of causation. However, a correlation does allow us to make predictions about one variable based on the other. For example, we can predict the number of reference questions and, therefore, the number of reference staff needed based on circulation.

11.2 The Mann-Whitney Test

The Mann-Whitney test is the nonparametric counterpart of the independent t test discussed in Chapter 9. As such, it can be used to test the hypothesis of difference between two unrelated populations when the data are in ordinal form. If the data are interval or ratio, but the requirements of a t test are not met (e.g., the frequency distributions are badly skewed), we can convert the data into ordinal form and then apply the Mann-Whitney test instead of the independent t test.

Suppose that ASIST wishes to establish whether there is a difference in incomes between male and female information professionals. ASIST randomly samples 80 of its members, 40 males and 40 females, and asks them to report their income figures anonymously. Since we are testing a mean difference in income figures, which are ratio data, and males and females are two independent groups, an independent t test would normally be applied. However, suppose it is known that the income distribution among information professionals is skewed, as income distribution is in the general population. Then the normality requirement of the t test is not met. Therefore the Mann-Whitney test, the nonparametric counterpart of the independent t test, should be used.

The null hypothesis for this test is that salaries for male and female information professionals are the same. The alternative hypothesis is that salaries are not the same. We will calculate a test statistic, the U score, from sample data and then decide whether to reject the null hypothesis or not based on the test statistic. Because U is the test statistic, some people call this test the Mann-Whitney U test.

The logic of the test statistic is fairly straightforward. For the convenience of discussion, suppose that we only have data from six people, three males and three females.

Male	Female
$44,000	$39,000
$55,000	$51,000
$59,999	$52,000

To calculate the test statistic, we will combine the two groups of data and then rank the combined data from low to high.

Income	Rank
44,000	2
55,000	5
59,000	6
39,000	1
51,000	3
52,000	4

The rankings for the male group are 2, 5, and 6 while those for the female group are 1, 3, and 4. If there is no difference between the two groups, then the average rankings of the groups should be similar. If there is a difference, then one group will have a significantly lower average ranking than the other group. The test statistic U evaluates the discrepancy in ranks between the two groups and indicates the probability of a significant difference between the two groups.

I will omit the details on how to calculate the U score because SPSS will do this for us. To do a Mann-Whitney test in SPSS, go through the following menu options: "Analyze," "Nonparametric Tests," "2 Independent Samples," and then specify the variables and select "Mann-Whitney U" in the popup screen. Figure 11-3 shows the output of the test.

Ranks

	Gender	N	Mean Rank	Sum of Ranks
Income	Male	40	47.99	1919.50
	Female	40	33.01	1320.50
	Total	80		

Test Statistics^a

	Income
Mann-Whitney U	500.500
Wilcoxon W	1320.500
Z	-2.882
Asymp. Sig. (2-tailed)	.004

a. Grouping Variable: Gender

Figure 11-3 SPSS Output of a Mann-Whitney Test

The first table of Figure 11-3 provides the basic information about the two groups being compared. There are 40 data points in each group (shown under the heading "N"). The average ranks of the two groups are 47.99 for males and 33.01 for females (under the heading "Mean Rank"). The sum of the ranking scores is 1,919.5 for the male group and 1,320.5 for the female group.[2] The Mann-Whitney U score is 500.5 as shown in the second table of Figure 11-3. We do not have to check a statistical table to find out the p-value for this U score because SPSS provides this number in its output. The p-value is listed as 0.004 in the line "Asymp. Sig. (two-tailed)." Because the p-value is less than 0.05, we can reject the null hypothesis and conclude that the income difference between male and female information professionals is statistically significant. As the average rank for the females is lower than that of the males (33.01 vs. 47.99), we can say that, at the group level, female information professionals have lower incomes than their male counterparts.

11.3 The Wilcoxon Signed Ranks Test

The Wilcoxon signed ranks test is the nonparametric equivalent to the paired t test discussed in Chapter 9. The Wilcoxon signed ranks test can be used when the paired t test was originally called for, but one or more requirements of the t test are not met. For example, you could use it in a case where the frequency distributions are badly skewed. **You may also see references to another Wilcoxon test called the Wilcoxon rank sum test. This is a different and unrelated test that is not discussed in this book. The Wilcoxon rank sum test is, in fact, related to the Mann-Whitney test discussed in the preceding section.**

The logic of the Wilcoxon signed ranks test is fairly straightforward. As an example, suppose that we are studying Internet use by children aged 10 to 14 and we want to find out if there is a difference between boys and girls in the amount of time they spend surfing the Web. Because factors such as family socio-economic status, parents' attitude toward children's use of the Web, and family computer facilities can affect the amount of time a child spends on the Web, we recruit families with both a boy and a girl to participate in the study. Ten families are selected. (This small sample size is used for the convenience of illustration. A larger sample size should be used in a real study.) Five families have a boy older than the girl and the other five families a girl older than the boy. The total amount of time (number of hours) each child spent on the Web in a week was recorded and the results are shown in the first three columns of Table 11-2.

Since the data collected, the number of hours, are ratio data and the two groups, boys and girls, are paired up by family, a paired t test would normally be used. However, a preliminary look at the data reveals that the frequency distribution of the two sets of data may be very skewed because there are a couple of families where the hours are much higher than the others. Therefore, the Wilcoxon signed ranks test will be applied.

Table 11-2   Illustration of the Wilcoxon Signed Ranks Test

Family	Boy	Girl	Difference between the boy and the girl (girl – boy)	Rank of difference	Signed rank
1	3.25	3.5	0.25	1	1
2	5.5	5	-0.5	2	-2
3	5	4.25	-0.75	3	-3
4	5	6	1	4	4
5	2.5	3.75	1.25	5	5
6	3.5	2	-1.5	6	-6
7	1	2.75	1.75	7	7
8	1.5	3.5	2	8	8
9	18	15.75	-2.25	9	-9
10	19	16.5	-2.5	10	-10

For this study, the null hypothesis states that there is no difference between boys and girls in the amount of time that they spend on surfing the Web. The alternative hypothesis says that there is a difference. To calculate the test statistic, we first calculate the difference score for each pair of data as shown in column 4 of Table 11-2 and then rank the difference scores from low to high ignoring the positive or negative signs (see column 5). Next we assign the positive or negative sign of the difference score back to the rank score as shown in column 6 (it should be clear now why this test is called "signed ranks test"). Finally, we add up all the positive signed rank scores in column 6, obtaining a total of 25, and do the same for the negative signed rank scores in column 6, which ends up with -30.

In each family, if the girl scored higher than the boy, then the rank score will be positive; if the girl scored lower than the boy, then the rank score will be negative. (Here, the difference score is calculated as the girl's score minus the boy's score. You can also define the difference score to be the boy's score minus the girl's score. This will change the positive and negative sign of the difference score but the test result will be the same.) If there is no significant difference between boys and girls on a group level, then the sum of the positive ranks and the sum of the negative ranks should be similar, as it is in this case. If there is a significant difference between boys and girls, then the sum of positive scores will be much larger than that of the negative scores or vice versa. The Wilcoxon test statistic can be calculated to evaluate the discrepancy between the two sum scores and thereby estimate the probability that the two groups under comparison, in this case boys and girls, are significantly different. I will omit the details on the actual calculation of the test statistic and the associated statistical table to use. (In fact, different books may show different formulae to calculate the test statistic as well as different statistical tables to use. However, the logic of the test is the same as discussed here.) We will again use SPSS to do the calculation. To perform a Wilcoxon signed ranks test in SPSS, go through menu options of "Analyze," "Nonparametric Tests," "2 Related Samples," and then specify the two groups of data being compared. Figure 11-4 is the SPSS output for the data in Table 11-2. The "Descriptive Statistics" listed at the end of the Figure is not included in the output by default. I appended these statistics to aid in a later discussion.

Wilcoxon Signed Ranks Test

Ranks

		N	Mean Rank	Sum of Ranks
GIRL - BOY	Negative Ranks	5a	6.00	30.00
	Positive Ranks	5b	5.00	25.00
	Ties	0c		
	Total	10		

a. GIRL < BOY

b. GIRL > BOY

c. BOY = GIRL

Test Statisticsb

	GIRL - BOY
Z	-.255a
Asymp. Sig. (2-tailed)	.799

a. Based on positive ranks.

b. Wilcoxon Signed Ranks Test

Descriptive Statistics

	N	Percentiles		
		25th	50th (Median)	75th
BOY	10	2.2500	4.2500	8.6250
GIRL	10	3.3125	4.0000	8.4375

Figure 11-4 SPSS Output of a Wilcoxon Signed Ranks Test

The first table of Figure 11-4 summarizes the ranking results. There are five negative ranking scores and five positive ranking scores. The sum of the negative ranking scores is 30 while that of the positive ranking scores is 25. This is the same as the result obtained through the manual calculations in Table 11-2. The second table of Figure 11-4 shows the test statistic, -0.255^3, and the associated p-value, 0.799. Because the p-value is greater than 0.05, we fail to reject the null hypothesis. This means that we have insufficient evidence from the data to prove that boys and girls spend different amounts of time surfing the Web. Using the median figures from the descriptive statistics included in Figure 11-4, we can see that, in fact, a typical boy spent 4.25 hours a week surfing the Web while a typical girl spent 4 hours a week. The minor difference of 0.25 hours (i.e., 15 minutes) is not statistically significant, meaning that there may not be a difference at all in the population.

11.4   Kruskal-Wallis Test

The Kruskal-Wallis test is the nonparametric equivalent to the one-way analysis of variance (ANOVA) discussed in Chapter 10. It can be used to determine if three or more unrelated groups of data under comparison are significantly different when the data are of ordinal type. If the data are of interval or ratio type but one or more requirements of ANOVA are not met, we can convert the data into ordinal form by ranking them and then apply the Kruskal-Wallis test. This may sound a lot like the Mann-Whitney test discussed earlier in this chapter. Indeed, the logic and the procedure of the two tests are similar other than the fact that the Mann-Whitney test compares two groups of data while the Kruskal-Wallis test compares three or more groups of data.

For an example to explain the logic and the procedure of the test, let us suppose that we are interested in knowing what affects children's ability to learn computer skills. We suspect that the presence of a home computer and the length of time it has been in the home make a difference. To test the hypothesis, we conduct an experiment in a school where we recruit 30 children from grade one. Ten of these children have no home computer; 10 of them have had a home computer for less than a year, and 10 of them have had a home computer for more than a year. The same instructor in the same instructional environment teaches all these children a set of computer skills new to them over a period of time. At the end of this period, a test is administered to all the children to see how well they learn the new skills taught. The test results are judged and ranked by a panel of experts. Table 11-3 shows the ranking result where a lower score means that the child learned the skills better; e.g., 1 is the best result while 30 is the worst result.

Table 11-3   Ranking Result of Computer Skills of Three Groups of Children

Have no home computer	Have a home computer for less than a year	Have a home computer for more than a year
13	2	1
15	3	4
16	5	9
18	6	10
21	7	11
24	8	12
25	17	14
26	19	20
28	27	22
30	29	23

Because the ranking scores are ordinal data and the three groups of children are independent of each other, a Kruskal-Wallis test is appropriate. Our null hypothesis is that there is no significant difference among the three groups of children in the ranking scores, which means that on a group level children learned the new computer skills equally well. The alternative hypothesis is that the three groups of children differ in how well they learned the new skills and thus the ranking scores of the three groups are not all the same; i.e., at least one group differs significantly from the other groups.

If the three groups of children are the same in their ability to learn new computer skills, then the total or average ranking scores for the three groups should be similar. On the other hand, if one or two groups learned better, than the total ranking score for that group(s) will be lower. The test statistic H evaluates the discrepancy of the ranking scores among the three groups. The larger the H score, the larger the discrepancy, making it more likely that the three groups are different, resulting in a smaller p-value (i.e., less probable that the null hypothesis is true). Statistical software packages such as SPSS will provide both the H score and the p-value in their output. To do the Kruskal-Wallis test in SPSS, go through the following menu options: "Analyze," "Nonparametric Tests," "K Independent Samples," and then specify variables and select "Kruskal-Wallis H" in the popup screen. The test result for data in Table 11-3 is shown in Figure 11-5.

Kruskal-Wallis Test

Ranks

	GROUP	N	Mean Rank
RANKING SCORE	no home computer	10	21.60
	less than a year	10	12.30
	more than a year	10	12.60
	Total	30	

Test Statistics[a,b]

	RANKING SCORE
Chi-Square	7.208
df	2
Asymp. Sig.	.027

a. Kruskal Wallis Test

b. Grouping Variable: GROUP

Figure 11-5   SPSS Output of a Kruskal-Wallis Test

The first table of Figure 11-5 shows the number of data points in each group (in the column with heading "N") and the average rank for each group (in the column with heading "Mean Rank"). Note that the average rank for the "no home computer" group is 21.6, much higher than that of the two other groups. Does this discrepancy in the ranking scores indicate a significant difference among the three groups? The Kruskal-Wallis test result in the second table of Figure 11-5 answers this question. The test statistic H is calculated at 7.208 (the number in the first line)[4] and the p-value for this test statistic is 0.027 (the number in the last line). Because the p-value is less than 0.05, we reject the null hypothesis and accept the alternative hypothesis.

The alternative hypothesis tells us that there is a significant difference among the three groups being compared. However, it does not specify the pattern of difference; i.e., whether one group differs from the other two groups or all three groups are different from each other. You may recall that after we find a significant difference among the groups under comparison in a one-way ANOVA, we can do a Tukey's HSD test to further determine the pattern of difference (see Section 10.4, Chapter 10). There are nonparametric counterpart tests that we can use to determine the pattern of difference after a Kruskal-Wallis test. A detailed discussion of these tests is beyond the scope of this book. Interested readers can refer to Conover (1980, 231–232) or Diekhoff (1996, 257–260).

For this particular test result, the pattern of difference is fairly clear even without a further test. Judging from the average rank scores of the three groups (see the last column in the first table of Figure 11-5), it is safe to say that the "no home computer" group is different from the other two groups because its average rank score is almost double that of the others. However, there is no significant difference between the "less than a year" group and the "more than a year" group because the average rank scores of these two groups are very close, 12.3 and 12.6 respectively. Summarizing the results of the study, we can say that children who have a home computer learn new computer skills better than children who do not have a home computer. However, whether the home computer has been available for more than a year or less than a year does not seem to affect children's ability to learn new computer skills. Care must be taken in interpreting the results of this study. The study only shows that children who have a home computer learn new computer skills better but it does not prove that it is the home computer itself that *caused* better ability to learn computer skills. Other factors such as socio-economic class of the family or the family's learning environment may dictate both the availability of a home computer and children's learning ability in general, not just the learning ability in computer skills.

The data in this example are ordinal data. As explained earlier, the Kruskal-Wallis test can also be used for interval or ratio data when one or more requirements of a one-way ANOVA are not met. The interval or ratio data should be converted into ordinal data before applying the Kruskal-Wallis test. The conversion is done by combining all groups of data together and then ranking the combined data from low to high or high to low. This is similar to the process used to convert interval or ratio data for the Mann-Whitney test. The Kruskal-Wallis test can then be applied to the ranking scores, which are ordinal data. If you are using SPSS, you do not have to do the conversion manually. Simply input the original interval or ratio data into SPSS and then run the Kruskal-Wallis test. SPSS will convert the data automatically and then produce the test result for you.

11.5   Advantages and Disadvantages of Nonparametric Tests

11.5.1   Advantages of Nonparametric Tests

The main advantage of nonparametric tests over parametric tests is that they do not impose certain requirements on the data, such as the normality or the homogeneity requirement. Parametric tests all have one or more of these requirements. If the requirement(s) are not met, but the parametric test is still used, the result may not be accurate. Nonparametric tests are also easier to calculate than their parametric counterparts but the use of computers to do all the calculations effectively eliminated this advantage. Now that we know nonparametric tests are less demanding on the quality of data, why do we still need parametric tests? Can we not just carry out the nonparametric counterpart test when a parametric test was originally called for? No, because nonparametric tests have disadvantages over their parametric counterparts.

11.5.2   Disadvantages of Nonparametric Tests

The first disadvantage of nonparametric tests is that their power is lower relative to their corresponding parametric tests. "Power" in statistics means the probability of finding a significant difference if there is one. Since nonparametric tests are less powerful, they are less likely to find a difference when in fact there is one. It is not difficult to understand why nonparametric tests are less powerful if you consider how data are processed. All nonparametric tests deal with ordinal data while all parametric tests deal with interval or ratio data. Ordinal data only contain information on greater than or less than while interval or ratio data contain more detailed information on how much greater than or how much less than. If the original data are of interval or ratio type, they are converted into ordinal type in a nonparametric test. The detailed information contained in the original interval or ratio data is lost in the conversion process. The less information we have, the less powerful the test becomes.

This point can be made clearer by a simple example. Suppose that you are comparing salaries for males and females. You have four male and female salary figures:

Male: $70,000, $60,000, $50,000, $49,000
Female: $61,000, $52,000, $51,000, $50,000

The average salary for males is $57,250 while that for females is $53,500, a difference of $3,750. However, if you rank all the eight data points, as is typically done in nonparametric tests, you will find no difference in the average rank. The first two males are ranked ahead of the first two females while the last two males are ranked behind the last two females, resulting an average rank of 4.5 for both groups. A close look at the data shows that when males are ranked ahead of females, the difference is at least $8,000. But when females are ahead, the difference is only $1,000. However, this detail on the amount of difference is lost in the ranking process and thus a nonparametric test will not detect the difference.

The second disadvantage attributed to nonparametric tests is that they are not very specific on the conclusions reached when a hypothesis of difference is tested. If the null hypothesis is rejected, we know that the populations under comparison are different but we do not know whether the difference is in central tendency, i.e., mean or median, or variability. However, the nonparametric tests discussed in this chapter are particularly sensitive to differences in central tendency (Howell, 1997, Conover, 1980) so we can reasonably assume that any difference found is in central tendency. In short, nonparametric tests place fewer restrictions on data but the results are also less specific. You get what you pay for.

11.5.3   When to Use a Nonparametric Test

If the data are of ordinal type, then you have no choice but to use a nonparametric test. If data are of interval or ratio type, then the general principle is to apply a parametric test unless the requirements of the parametric test are grossly not met. For example, if we plan to do a t test but find that the frequency distributions are somewhat skewed, we can still conduct the t test unless the frequency distributions are highly skewed. The parametric tests discussed in the proceeding chapters are fairly robust, which means that moderate deviations of data from the requirements of the test will not have severe consequences for the accuracy of the result. T tests and ANOVA are particularly robust if the sample sizes for the groups being compared are equal and fairly large (Agresti and

Finlay, 1997, 186–187, 473–474). The fact that a parametric test is, in general, more powerful than its corresponding nonparametric test makes the former the preferred test when it is reasonable to use it.

Endnotes

1. The data used in this example were from the 1996 Ontario Library Statistics.

2. You may wonder why there are decimal points for the rank scores in the SPSS output. This occurs when there are ties in the rank; i.e., two or more data points have the same value so their ranking positions are the same. SPSS breaks the tie by assigning the average rank score to the tied data points. For example, if the original data are 10, 20, 20, 30, then the rank scores will be 1, 2.5, 2.5, 4.

3. You may find that some books say that the test statistic should be a T score rather than the Z score as shown in the SPSS output here. The issue of which test statistic to use in a given situation is a little complex and beyond the scope of this book. If you are doing the test using a software package, you do not have to worry about this problem.

4. You may wonder why the test statistic H is labeled as "Chi-Square" in the SPSS output. This is because the sampling distribution of H approximately follows the chi-square distribution with k-1 degrees of freedom where k is the number of groups being compared. Do not worry about this technical detail if you find it confusing. We do not have to concern ourselves with these details in order to use the test.

CHAPTER 12

When Should I Use Which Test?—A Road Map

After reading the preceding chapters, you may find that the individual statistical tests are not difficult to understand or to use. This is exactly what this book tries to convey. However, the number of statistical tests available may seem overwhelming, especially when you have to decide which test to apply in a particular situation. In my experience supervising student projects, the selection of appropriate tests is usually the biggest hurdle for beginners. Once students get past this step, they have no problem actually doing the tests because computer software can do all the calculations. They just have to interpret the results. How do we decide which test to use in the first place? This chapter will provide the answer.

In Figure 12-1, I have summarized all the statistical tests discussed so far into two charts. These charts are designed to serve as a road map that will guide you to the appropriate statistical test for a given situation. For each test listed in Figure 12-1, I indicated the chapter in which the test is discussed in order to make it easier for you to refer back once you have selected a test.

When following this road map to decide which test to use, you must first determine which type of hypothesis you are testing. All statistical tests we have discussed so far deal with either hypothesis of association or hypothesis of difference. Hypothesis of association appears in the top part of Figure 12-1 and hypothesis of difference is in the lower part. If you want to test a theory that says two variables are related, then you are testing a hypothesis of association. For example, if you suspect that a person's attitude to children surfing on the Internet is related to their gender or that library circulation is related to collection size, then you are dealing with a hypothesis of association. By contrast, the hypothesis of difference says that there is a difference between or among groups being compared. For example, if you are testing to see whether funding levels of public libraries in the United States are higher than those in Canada, then you are testing a hypothesis of difference.

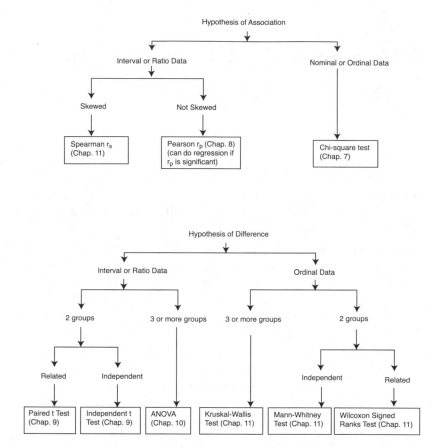

Figure 12-1 A Road Map for Finding the Correct Statistical Test

If you are testing a hypothesis of association, go to the top of Figure 12-1 and find "Hypothesis of Association." You must then decide what type of data you have. Both variables must be of the appropriate data type in order to proceed along a branch of the Figure. That is, to go in the "Nominal or Ordinal" direction, both variables must be of nominal or ordinal type. In the example of testing for a relationship between gender and attitude toward children surfing the Internet, if you measure attitude using a scale of 1 to 5 (Pro to Anti) then the attitude data are ordinal data. Gender is always nominal data. Therefore, according to Figure 12-1, you should do a chi-square test because the data are either nominal or ordinal for both variables. In the second example, determining whether library circulation is linked to library collection size, both circulation and collection size are ratio data.

Following the "Interval or Ratio Data" branch of the chart, you can apply either the Spearman correlation coefficient test or the Pearson correlation coefficient test depending on how skewed the frequency distributions of the two variables are. As discussed in Chapter 11, we can still use the Pearson correlation coefficient test if the distributions are a little skewed. The Spearman correlation coefficient test is used only when one or both distributions are badly skewed. How do you know what the frequency distribution looks like for a given data set? Simply do a histogram for the data set as discussed in Chapter 3, Section 3.2.

If you are testing a hypothesis of difference, find "Hypothesis of Difference" in the middle of Figure 12-1. As with hypothesis of association, the next thing to decide is the type of data you have. Suppose that you want to determine whether there is a difference in the funding level between the U.S. public libraries and the Canadian public libraries. You randomly sampled 50 public libraries from each country and collected their funding data in dollar figures. You decided that this is a hypothesis of difference and arrived at the lower part of Figure 12-1. Funding data here are apparently ratio data so you proceed to the left branch of the chart. Since you are comparing two groups, U.S. vs. Canada, you further moved down to the "2 groups" side of the chart. The question now is whether or not the two groups are related.[1] It is fairly clear that the two groups are independent of each other (a particular U.S. library is not related to a particular Canadian library), so you should do an independent t test.

Before you actually carry out the independent t test, you should check to see if the requirements of the test are met. To check the normality requirement, do a histogram for both the U.S data and the Canadian data to see whether or not the frequency distributions are approximately normal. The homogeneity requirement can be checked by comparing the standard deviations of the two groups of data. If, for example, the standard deviations of the two groups of data are very different, say five times different, then the homogeneity requirement is not met. The Mann-Whitney test, the nonparametric counterpart of the independent t test, should be used. If you do not remember which nonparametric test is the counterpart of a given parametric test, the "Hypothesis of Difference" chart of Figure 12-1 can still help. Go to the "Ordinal Data" branch because the ratio data will be converted into ordinal data when applying the nonparametric test. Now follow the path to "2 groups" and "Independent," as we have decided that the data belong to this type. The conclusion you will reach is that you should use a Mann-Whitney test.

There is an even easier way of reaching this conclusion. The two branches of the "Hypothesis of Difference" chart ("interval or ratio data" vs. "ordinal data") are designed to be mirror images of each other. To find the nonparametric counterpart of the independent t test, just look for its mirror image in the other branch and you will find the Mann-Whitney test. This method will also lead you from ANOVA to its counterpart, the Kruskal-Wallis test, and from the paired t test to the Wilcoxon signed ranks test. Before carrying out a paired t test or ANOVA, you also need to check to see if the requirements of the test are met.

Years ago, a Canadian public library conducted a survey in the community it served. One of the questions in the survey asked about the number of books the respondent read in a month. The survey also asked about the highest level of education attained and provided public school, high school, and post secondary as the possible answers. Suppose that we want to find out whether people with more education read more books. What statistical test should we do? In consulting Figure 12-1, first we have to decide what type of hypothesis we are testing. It looks like a hypothesis of difference because our question can be worded as "are the number of books read by these three groups of people the same or different." The data collected from the question "number of books read" are of ratio type. Because we are comparing three groups of ratio data, according to Figure 12-1 we should use ANOVA if the requirements of ANOVA are met.

However, some people may argue that it is a hypothesis of association because we can word the question we are trying to answer as "Is the number of books a person reads related to his/her education level?" The data collected on the variable education level are ordinal data and the data for the number of books read are ratio data. Looking at the "Hypothesis of Association" chart of Figure 12-1, we may feel that we cannot proceed to either branch because we have a mixture of ordinal data (right branch) and ratio data (left branch). As discussed in Chapter 1, Section 1.5, we cannot convert ordinal data into ratio data. However, we can convert ratio data into ordinal data. For example, we can classify number of books read into groups of 0-2, 3-5, 6-8, and 9 or more. Now that both variables are of ordinal type, we can proceed to the right branch of the "Hypothesis of Association" chart, which leads to the decision to use a chi-square test. When I asked my students to analyze this survey data as an assignment, there were people who converted the data this way and then did a chi-square test.

We must now decide whether ANOVA or a chi-square test is better in this case. I recommend the former because, as discussed in Chapter 11, Section 11.5, parametric tests such as ANOVA are more powerful than nonparametric tests such as the chi-square test and are therefore more likely to reject a wrong null hypothesis. For the example data discussed here, ANOVA revealed a significant difference in the number of books read among the three groups of people being compared. A Tukey's HSD test further revealed that the difference comes from the group with post secondary education. On average, this group of people read more books than people in the two other groups. However, a chi-square test did not show that the number of books read is related to education level. As discussed in Chapter 1, Section 1.5, ratio data contain more information than ordinal data do. The more information we have, the better statistical decision we can make. As a general principle, do not convert interval or ratio data into ordinal data to do a nonparametric test unless the requirements of a parametric test are grossly not met.

As a final note, I would like to emphasize that Figure 12-1 is a summary of the basic statistical tests discussed in this book. As such, it does not cover all the tests available, nor does it include all the issues we have to consider in the choice of a correct test. For example, when testing a hypothesis of difference involving two groups of data, the chart tells us to consider whether or not the two groups are related and then apply the corresponding test. For a comparison among three or more groups, however, the chart does not show that we have to consider the issue of whether or not the groups are related. Theoretically, we still have to consider this issue. As a matter of fact, ANOVA and the Kruskal-Wallis test are both for situations where the groups being compared are not related, the more commonly encountered situation. If the groups are related, then we should use repeated measure ANOVA instead of the ordinary ANOVA discussed in this book, and the Friedman test instead of the Kruskal-Wallis test. These tests are not usually covered in basic statistics books. They are also relatively rare in information science or in social science in general. Interested readers can refer to other books such as Howell (1997).

Endnote

1. Please refer to Chapter 9, Section 9.1, if you do not remember how to judge whether or not the two groups are related.

CHAPTER 13

Getting Sophisticated—A Taste of Some Advanced Statistical Methods

Various statistical methods have been used in information science research. These range from basic methods, such as those discussed in the preceding chapters, to more advanced ones. There is no strict definition dividing basic methods from more advanced methods. Generally speaking, basic statistical methods involve fewer variables, usually one independent variable and one dependent variable. By contrast, intermediate and advanced methods deal with more variables. Once you understand the basic methods, it is not difficult to extend your understanding to intermediate and advanced ones because the logic behind all the statistical tests is similar. A complete discussion of all the intermediate and advanced methods is beyond the scope of this book. This chapter will give you a taste of these statistical techniques by discussing three methods: two-way ANOVA, multiple regression, and LISREL. Two-way ANOVA and multiple regression are the most commonly used intermediate statistical methods. LISREL is an advanced method. It can be viewed as an extension of multiple regression so it serves to illustrate how statistical methods evolve.

13.1 Two-Way ANOVA

Two-way ANOVA, short for two-way analysis of variance, is an extension to one-way ANOVA discussed in Chapter 10. If you look back at the examples in Chapter 10, you will find that there is only one factor, or independent variable, that affects the dependent variable. This is why we call it one-way ANOVA. Two-way ANOVA, on the other hand, can investigate the effects of two independent variables on the dependent variable. The following example illustrates how to choose the appropriate type of ANOVA. Suppose that you are studying salary differences among information profession-als. If you want to test the hypothesis that the level of education received affects one's salary, then you have one dependent vari-able, salary, and one independent variable, education. If education is measured by the highest degree (bachelor, master, or doctoral) one received and salary is measured in dollar figures, then a one-way ANOVA can be used to analyze the data.[1] If you think that gen-der is a factor in salary and want to include this factor in your study too, then you have two independent variables: education and gen-der. You need to use a two-way ANOVA.

As you can imagine, there are situations where you want to study the effects of three or more factors on a dependent variable. Three-way ANOVA or higher-order ANOVA are designed for these situations. Two-way and higher-order ANOVA are called factorial ANOVA as there are multiple factors involved. I will limit the discussion here to two-way ANOVA, since the basic methods and principles of higher-order ANOVA are the same.

You may wonder why we need to learn a new statistical test, the two-way ANOVA, to study effects of two factors, Can we not do a sep-arate one-way ANOVA for each factor? No, because two-way ANOVA has several advantages over two separate one-way ANOVA. Therefore, it should always be used when dealing with multiple factors. The main advantage is that factorial ANOVA allows us to study interac-tions between or among factors. I will discuss how to examine inter-actions later but I would first like to use an example in information science research to illustrate the importance of knowing the interac-tions among different variables.

Many studies have been carried out to investigate user perform-ance in information retrieval systems. Factors that have been consid-ered to have an effect on user behavior include search experience and other individual differences such as gender. However, these studies often investigated different factors separately and therefore failed to reveal how factors interact with each other. When I conducted an information retrieval experiment in a hypertext system and analyzed the data by a factorial ANOVA, I did find that there may be an inter-action between two variables: search experience and gender. This interaction would not be found and examined if I studied the two fac-tors separately using two one-way ANOVA. The study was reported in the *Canadian Journal of Information and Library Science* (Qiu, 1993). The example I will use in the following explanation of two-way

ANOVA is adapted from this study. Data were modified for the convenience of discussion.

The study was conducted during 1990 and 1991 when hypertext information retrieval systems were just appearing commercially. Hypertext systems allow users to find information by browsing; i.e., following links between items, as well as by traditional keyword searching (the World Wide Web is an example of hypertext). The purpose of the study was to investigate which method (analytical searching vs. browsing) users preferred for searching hypertext systems. For the experimental system used in the study, analytical searching was defined as keyword searching with or without Boolean operators. Subjects were asked to conduct a search on the experimental system. Their search processes were automatically logged and later played back for analysis. It was found that all subjects used a combination of analytical searching and browsing to find the information stored in the hypertext nodes (a node is a unit of information in a hypertext system, e.g., a single page in a Web site). However, some subjects used more analytical searching than others did. The pattern of each search (analytical vs. browsing) was measured by the percentage of nodes reached through analytical searching. I wanted to find out if the subjects' gender and search experience affected their search patterns. Therefore, the dependent variable was search pattern and the independent variables were subjects' gender and search experience. A two-way ANOVA was used to analyze the data. The following three null hypotheses were tested:

- There is no significant difference between males and females in search pattern as measured by percent of nodes reached through analytical searching.
- There is no significant difference between experienced users and novice users in search pattern as measured by percent of nodes reached through analytical searching.
- There is no significant interaction between the two variables of gender and search experience.

The basic logic of two-way ANOVA is the same as that of one-way ANOVA: determine whether there is a significant mean difference by analyzing the variability. In one-way ANOVA, as you may recall from Chapter 10, we first calculate an F score, which is the ratio of between group variability over within group variability. We then determine the p-value, the probability for the null hypothesis to be true, based on the F score. If the p-value is equal to or less than the pre-set significance level, usually 0.05, we will reject the null hypothesis. On the other hand, if the p-value is greater than 0.05 we will fail to reject the null hypothesis.

The same procedure is followed in two-way ANOVA. The difference is that we will calculate three F scores because we have three null hypotheses to be tested. For each null hypothesis, we will decide whether or not to reject it based on the corresponding F score. As in one-way ANOVA, the F score is a ratio of between group variability over within group variability. As usual, we do not have to worry about the mathematical details of how to calculate the variability

Between-Subjects Factors

		Value Label	N
Gender	1	male	30
	2	female	30
Experience	1	novice	30
	2	experienced	30

Descriptive Statistics

Dependent Variable: search pattern

Gender	Experience	Mean	Std. Deviation	N
male	novice	.2633	.1314	15
	experienced	.5300	.1678	15
	Total	.3967	.2008	30
female	novice	.3347	.1188	15
	experienced	.1767	.1147	15
	Total	.2557	.1401	30
Total	novice	.2990	.1283	30
	experienced	.3533	.2285	30
	Total	.3262	.1858	60

Tests of Between-Subjects Effects

Dependent Variable: search pattern

Source	Type III Sum of Squares	df	Mean Square	F	Sig.
Corrected Model	1.019a	3	.340	18.691	.000
Intercept	6.383	1	6.383	351.325	.000
GENDER	.298	1	.298	16.414	.000
EXPERIEN	4.428E-02	1	4.428E-02	2.437	.124
GENDER * EXPERIEN	.676	1	.676	37.223	.000
Error	1.017	56	1.817E-02		
Total	8.419	60			
Corrected Total	2.036	59			

a. R Squared = .500 (Adjusted R Squared = .474)

Figure 13-1   A SPSS Output of Two-Way ANOVA

because we will resort to a computer program to do the calculations. I will interpret the SPSS output, shown in Figure 13-1 and Figure 13-2, for the above study to further explain the meaning of two-way ANOVA (the SPSS output is too long to fit into one figure, so it is broken into two figures).

Profile Plots

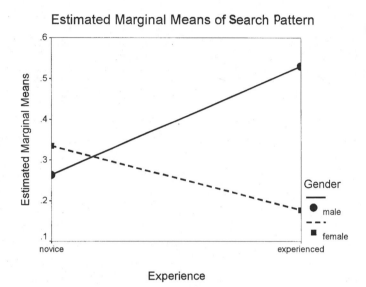

Figure 13-2   A SPSS Output of Two-Way ANOVA (continued)

The first table in Figure 13-1 shows the two independent variables involved, gender and experience (i.e., search experience). Each variable has two categories with 30 subjects in each category (e.g., there are 30 males and 30 females). It should be pointed out that there are a total of 60 subjects, not 120 subjects as it may appear from the SPSS output. The second table shows the number of subjects in each combination of the two variables and the associated means (averages). For example, the first line of the table shows that there are 15 male subjects who are novice searchers and their mean search pattern score (the dependent variable) is 0.2633. It will be clearer if we organize the mean scores into a table as shown in Table 13-1.

There are four possible combinations for the two independent variables as represented by the four shaded cells in Table 13-1. There are 15 subjects in each cell and the mean search pattern score of the

15 subjects is listed in the cell. The last column in Table 13-1 shows the means for the variable search experience regardless of gender. For example, the mean for all the novice users, male and female combined, is 0.2990. Similarly, the last row of Table 13-1 shows the means for the variable gender regardless of search experience.

Table 13-1   Summary of Mean Scores of Search Pattern

	Male	Female	Group Average
Novice	0.2633	0.3347	0.2990
Experienced	0.5300	0.1767	0.3533
Group Average	0.3967	0.2557	0.3262

The third table of Figure 13-1 summarizes the two-way ANOVA result with the F score and the associated p-value for each null hypothesis being tested. For example, the line labeled as "GENDER" shows that the F score for the gender factor (the first null hypothesis stated above) is 16.414 and the p-value is less than 0.05 (the p-value is listed in the last column under the heading "Sig."). Therefore, we can reject the null hypothesis and conclude that males and females do differ in search pattern. As shown in Table 13-1, the average search pattern score for males is 0.3967, higher than 0.2557 for the females.

The F score for the search experience factor (the second null hypothesis stated above) is 2.437 and the associated p-value is 0.124 (see the line labeled as "EXPERIEN" in the third table of Figure 13-1). So we fail to reject the null hypothesis and conclude that there is insufficient evidence from this study to prove that search experience affects search pattern. Table 13-1 shows that the average search pattern score for the experienced users is 0.3533, fairly close to the 0.2990 for novice users. This small difference among the sample subjects of the study is not statistically significant, suggesting no difference exists in the population.

The third null hypothesis tested refers to the interaction between the two factors of gender and search experience. The F score for this hypothesis is 37.223 and the p-value is less than 0.05 (see the line labeled as "GENDER * EXPERIEN" in the third table of Figure 13-1). Thus we reject the null hypothesis and conclude that the two factors do interact with each other. In general, interaction of two variables means that the effect of one variable is different at different levels of the other variable. In this particular case, interaction means that the gender effect (one variable) is different for novice users as opposed to the experienced users (different levels of the other variable).

The meaning of this interaction will be clearer if we look at the graph presented as Figure 13-2. This graph plots the four mean scores of search pattern (male novice, male experienced, female novice, and female experienced). The vertical axis represents search pattern, the dependent variable. The horizontal axis represents search experience, the independent variable. The two lines, one for males and the other for females, represent the variable gender. The fact that the two lines are not parallel shows that there is an interaction of the two variables. For novice users, females scored higher while for experienced users, males scored higher. If there were no interaction, then one line should be higher than the other for both novice and experienced users, resulting in two parallel lines.

Summarizing the results for the three hypotheses, we can say that gender affects search pattern in that males are more likely to use analytical searching while females are more likely to use browsing. Search experience alone does not affect search pattern. However, search experience does interact with the gender factor such that the gender effect is more pronounced among experienced users than novice users. The fact that the two gender lines are very close to each other at the novice end of the graph suggests that the gender difference among novice users is not statistically significant, although it appears that female novices are more likely to use analytical search. There is a further test called test of simple effect that we can do to prove that the gender difference among novice users is not statistically significant. This test is beyond the scope of this book, but interested readers can refer to Howell (1997, 412–415).

A graph like the one in Figure 13-2 is a very common and useful tool to examine the interactions in factorial ANOVA. The graph always has the dependent variable on the vertical axis. It does not matter which independent variable is placed on the horizontal axis and which one is represented by separate lines. Regardless of which variable is placed on the horizontal axis, the lines will be parallel or almost parallel to each other if there is no interaction between variables and non-parallel if there is an interaction. For example, in the graph of Figure 13-2, the search experience variable is placed on the horizontal axis and the gender variable represented by the two separate lines. We can reverse the positions of the two variables by placing gender variable on the horizontal axis as shown in Figure 13-3. The pattern of the graph is unchanged in that the two lines still cross each other.

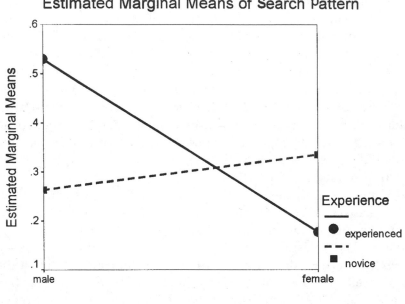

Figure 13-3   A Graph Showing Interaction of Variables

The example that I have used so far in the discussion involves two independent variables with each variable having two levels (male and female for gender; novice users and experienced users for search experience), so it is called a 2x2 factorial design. If we classify subjects' search experience into three levels of novice, intermediate, and expert, then we will have a 2x3 factorial design. We will still use a two-way ANOVA to analyze the data because we still have two independent variables. If this two-way ANOVA shows that the search experience has a significant effect on the search pattern, i.e., the three experience groups differ in search pattern, then we can use a Tukey's HSD test to find out the pattern of difference, as we did in one-way ANOVA. You can use SPSS to do this test too.

13.2 Multiple Regression

13.2.1 Why Do We Need Multiple Regression?

Multiple regression is an extension of simple regression, which was discussed in Chapter 8. Simple regression deals with only two variables, one dependent variable and one independent variable. For this reason, it is also called bivariate (two variable) regression. Multiple regression extends bivariate regression by allowing multiple (two or more) independent variables. However there is still only one dependent variable. I will use data collected in one of my research projects to explain why we need multiple regression and the basic concepts of multiple regression. For the convenience of discussion, the example in this chapter involves only two independent variables. However, the theory and principles can be easily applied to situations involving three or more independent variables.

The data I will use in the example come from an investigation of the preparedness of Canadian federal depository libraries for the transition to electronic access to government information (Dolan and Vaughan, 1998). Among the data that libraries were asked to report were the number of PCs (personal computers) the library has, the number of staff, and the size of the library's collection. The results revealed great variability among libraries in the number of PCs owned. Not surprisingly, the number of PCs is correlated with the number of staff employed. The Pearson correlation coefficient is 0.647 for public libraries in the survey, representing a statistically significant relationship. Thus we can develop a regression equation to predict the number of PCs based on staff size. The regression equation is:

$$Y = 10.85 + 0.29X$$

In this equation Y is the number of PCs and X is the staff size. The coefficient of determination is 0.419 (square of correlation coefficient), meaning that 41.9 percent of the variation in the number of PCs among the public libraries can be attributed to, or explained by, the variation in the staff size.

It makes sense that the number of PCs is related to staff size, as a larger staff will need more computers. However, staff size only explains 41.9 percent, not 100 percent, of the variation. Common sense tells us that other factors, or variables, also affect the number of

PCs a library has. One possible factor seems to be the collection size (the total number of items the library has). A calculation of the correlation coefficient between number of PCs and the collection size turned out to be 0.632, which is also statistically significant. The coefficient of determination, R squared, is 0.399. This means that 39.9 percent of the variation in the number of PCs can be explained by the variation in the collection size. Everything we have done so far is simple regression as discussed in Chapter 8.

It might to tempting to conclude that the two variables, staff size and collection size, together explain 81.8 percent (41.9 percent + 39.9 percent) of the variation in the number of PCs. However, this is incorrect because these two variables are related to each other, so that their contributions to the dependent variable overlap. A public library with a larger collection will have a larger staff; very likely because it serves a larger population. Because staff size and collection size are correlated, part of the variation in the number of PCs explained by staff size is also explained by collection size and vice versa. When we analyze the effect of two or more factors (independent variables) on a dependent variable, we cannot analyze each factor separately and then simply add the results together, because by doing so we will count the overlapping portion of the effect twice. Instead, we need to use multiple regression, which analyzes all the variables together and takes into consideration the overlaps, or interactions, among the independent variables.

13.2.2 *Multiple Regression Equation*

Before continuing the discussion on coefficient of determination, I will first introduce the structure of a multiple regression equation. Recall from Chapter 8 that the equation for simple regression is $Y = a + bX$ where Y is the dependent variable and X is the independent variable. Regression coefficients a and b are the intercept and the slope respectively for the regression line. The equation for multiple regression is similar in structure with extra independent variables added to the right side of the equation. So the multiple regression equation involving two independent variables is:

$$Y = b_0 + b_1X_1 + b_2X_2$$

where Y is dependent variable and X_1 and X_2 are the two independent variables.[2] Coefficient b_0 is the intercept, equivalent to coefficient a in the simple regression equation. Coefficients b_1 and b_2 are the slopes for X_1 and X_2 respectively, similar to coefficient b in the simple regression equation.

To develop a multiple regression equation we just have to calculate regression coefficients from the data collected, the same as in simple regression. However, the calculation of the coefficients for multiple regression is much more complicated than that for simple regression so we almost always use a computer to do the job. I will use SPSS to analyze the above data and demonstrate how to interpret the SPSS output shown in Figure 13-4. Although multiple regression only introduces one or more independent variables in comparison to simple regression, it is much more complicated than simple regression and involves more issues that are beyond the scope of this book. Part of the SPSS output is related to those issues so I have omitted them in Figure 13-4.

Model Summary

Model	R	R Square	Adjusted R Square	Std. Error of the Estimate
1	.750[a]	.562	.556	33.1749

a. Predictors: (Constant), collection, staff

Coefficients[a]

Model		Unstandardized Coefficients		Standardized Coefficients	t	Sig.	Correlations		
		B	Std. Error	Beta			Zero-order	Partial	Part
1	(Constant)	8.805	3.029		2.907	.004			
	staff	.202	.027	.453	7.371	.000	.647	.519	.402
	collection	2.389E-05	.000	.425	6.922	.000	.632	.496	.378

a. Dependent Variable: Number of PCs

Figure 13-4 Part of a SPSS Output of Multiple Regression

13.2.3 Regression Coefficients

Figure 13-4 consists of two tables. The second table contains the regression coefficients. The first column of the table lists "(constant)," which is b_0, and the names of the two independent variables "staff" and "collection." The second column lists the actual coefficients b_0, b_1, and b_2, which are 8.8, 0.2, and 0.000024 respectively. (2.389E-05 equals 0.00002389. This is a common number format in computer programs.) So the multiple regression equation is:

$$Y = 8.8 + 0.2X_1 + 0.000024X_2$$

where X_1 and X_2 represent staff size and collection size respectively.

We can use the multiple regression equation to predict the dependent variable given different values of independent variables. To do this, we simply plug the X_1 and X_2 values into the equation and then calculate the Y value. For example, a library with a staff size of 10 and collection size of 100,000 would have approximately 13.2 PCs (8.8 + 0.2×10 + 0.000024×100,000 = 13.2). Another library with a staff of 11 and collection size of 100,000 would have approximately 13.4 PCs. I use the word "approximately" here because a prediction based on the regression equation is not 100 percent accurate, an issue that was discussed in simple regression.

Note that the two predictions of the number of PCs are 0.2 apart and that this is the same as the regression coefficient for X_1 (the staff size). Also note that the collection sizes in the two predictions do not change while the staff size is increased by 1 in the second prediction. This illustrates the meaning of regression coefficient b_1 for X_1: If we increase one unit on the independent variable X_1 while holding the value of other variables (in this case the collection size) constant, the amount of increase in the dependent variable would be b_1. The same applies to b_2 for X_2 (collection size). If the collection size were increased by one unit while the staff size remained the same, the expected increase in the number of PCs would be 0.000024. You may wonder why the collection size has so little effect on the number of PCs compared with that of the staff size. This is because library collection sizes are often in the range of hundreds of thousands or even millions. An increase of one item in the collection is not noticeable. If we measure the collection size by units of 100,000, then an increase of one unit would have more effect on the dependent variable. In fact, the regression coefficient b_2 (collection size) would be 2.4, greater than the value of 0.2 for b_1 (staff size).

13.2.4   *Multiple Correlation Coefficient and Multiple Coefficient of Determination*

The multiple correlation coefficient R is the counterpart to the Pearson correlation coefficient r in simple regression. It indicates the strength of relationship between the dependent variable and the set of independent variables. The value of R ranges between zero and one with zero indicating no relationship and one indicating a perfect relationship. The closer the R value is to one, the stronger the relationship. Figure 13-4 shows the R to be 0.75 for this data set (see the second column of the first table), representing a fairly strong relationship.

The third column of the first table in Figure 13-4 lists the R-squared, which is calculated as the square of R. It is the counterpart to the coefficient of determination in simple regression so it is called the multiple coefficient of determination. As such, its meaning is equivalent to that of coefficient of determination in simple regression. It tells us the proportion of variation in the dependent variable that can be attributed to, or explained by, the set of independent variables. Figure 13-4 shows the R-squared to be 0.562. So we can say that 56.2 percent of the variation in the number of PCs among public libraries can be explained by the combination of variations in staff size and collection size. As discussed earlier, if we do two simple regressions for staff size and collection size separately and then add the two coefficients of determination together, we will get 81.8 percent. Now the multiple regression shows that the two independent variables together explain 56.2 percent of the dependent variable. This 25.6 percent reduction (81.8 percent minus 56.2 percent) is due to the overlap between the two independent variables.

13.2.5 Partial Correlation Coefficient

We have established that the simple correlation coefficient between the number of PCs and staff size overestimates the true relationship between them because it contains the effect of the third variable, collection size. Is there a more accurate measure of association between two variables that can rule out the effect of the third variable? Yes, there is and it is called the partial correlation coefficient, an important concept in multiple regression. "Partial correlation coefficient gives a single measure of association between two variables, taking into consideration the presence of one or more other variables. That is, partial correlation provides a single measure of association between two variables while adjusting for the effect of one or more other variables" (Walsh, 1990, 263). Like the Pearson correlation coefficient, the value of partial correlation coefficient falls between -1 and +1. A larger absolute value of the partial correlation coefficient indicates a stronger relationship between the two variables with the effects of other variables partialled out (removed).

The calculation of the partial correlation coefficient is fairly elaborate so we will once again resort to using the computer output. We can find partial correlation coefficients in the second table of Figure 13-4. They are listed in the second to last column with the heading "partial." So the partial correlation coefficient between the number of PCs and staff size is 0.519. This is a measure of association between the number of PCs and staff size with the effect of collection size partialled out. In other words, for a group of libraries with the same collection size, the simple correlation coefficient between the number of PCs and staff size would be 0.519. Similar interpretation applies to the partial correlation coefficient between the number of PCs and the collection size with the effect of staff size partialled out. Figure 13-4 shows this coefficient to be 0.496.

The two partial correlation coefficients here are called first-order partial correlation coefficients because we only removed, or controlled for, the effect of one other variable. If we want to control for the effect of two or more other variables, then we need to calculate second-order or higher-order partial correlation coefficients. This topic is beyond the scope of this book. Interested readers can refer to more advanced statistics books such as Agresti and Finlay (1997, 414–415).

13.3 LISREL

LISREL is an acronym for the LInear Structural RELations model. It can be considered as an extension of path analysis, which can, in turn, be viewed as an extension of multiple regression. In multiple regression, as was just discussed in the previous section of this chapter, there is one dependent variable and multiple independent variables. Path analysis (not covered in this book) involves multiple independent variables and multiple dependent variables. Like path analysis, LISREL can have multiple independent and dependent variables. In addition, it uses both observed and latent variables, two concepts that will be discussed in detail in the next paragraph. Because of these characteristics, LISREL can be used to analyze more complex problems than either multiple regression or path analysis.

To explain observed and latent variables, let us first look at the variables involved in multiple or simple regression. The variables that we deal with in regression analysis are called observed variables because they can be directly observed or measured and we can collect data on them. In fact, all of the variables that we have encountered so far in this book are observed variables. LISREL involves a new type of variable called the latent variable. In contrast to observed variables, latent variables cannot be measured or observed directly, nor can we collect data on them. Instead, they are formulated in terms of theoretical or hypothetical concepts. For example, we cannot directly observe or measure business success, nor can we collect data on it. Therefore, business success is a latent variable. By contrast, we can measure profit by dollar figures and we can collect profit data on a business. Therefore, profit is an observed variable. In a LISREL model, each latent variable is represented or measured by one or more observed variables and we collect data on the observed variables. For instance, profit could be used as one of the observed variables for the latent variable business success.

I will use the LISREL model developed in one of my research projects to explain the basic concepts of LISREL. The project was an attempt to quantitatively measure the impact (or contribution) of information, relative to other factors, on business success. We hypothesised that business success depends on the business environment, business development, and the use of business information. In other words, business success is the dependent variable and business environment, business development, and use of information are the independent variables. All of these variables are latent variables. The observed variables used to measure each of these latent variables will be discussed later.

A LISREL model is typically expressed by a path diagram such as the one shown in Figure 13-5, which is the model developed in our study. Dependent variables are shown on the right side of the diagram and the independent variables on the left side. Lower case letters inside circles indicate latent variables. Arrows point from the independent variables to the dependent variables to show that the former affects the latter. So, the model in Figure 13-5 states that the variables **busienvi** (business environment), **develop** (business development), and **info_use** (use of information) affect, or contribute to, **success** (business success). Please note that variable names are indicated by boldface throughout this discussion.

All four latent variables in Figure 13-5 are measured by two or more observed variables that are indicated by upper case letters inside boxes. Arrows point from the latent variable to the corresponding observed variables. For example, the latent variable **success** (business success) is measured by observed variables **FIXED** (fixed assets), **LIQUID** (liquid assets), **SALES** (sales), **PROFIT** (profit), and **PROSPECT** (the prospects of the business). Similarly, the latent variable **busienvi** (business environment) is measured by observed variables **FINANCE** (availability of financing) and **LOCATION** (location of the business). The latent variable **develop** (business development) is measured by **TECHNOLO** (technological development) and **MARKET** (market development). Finally, the latent variable **info_use** (use of information) is measured by **INFORMAL** (use of various informal information) and **FORMAL** (the use of various formal information). In this study, formal information refers to recorded information from such sources as electronic databases, libraries, newspapers, and government documents while informal information refers to information obtained through communication with friends and colleagues.

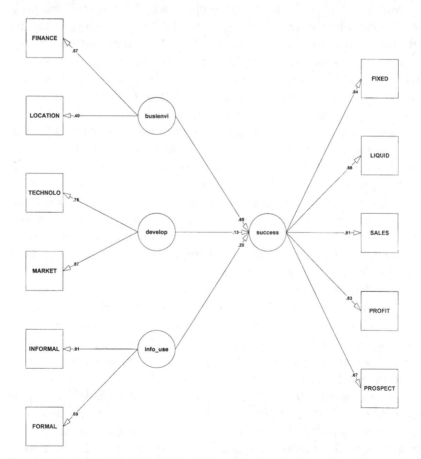

Figure 13-5 LISREL Model Studying Factors Affecting Business Success

In Figure 13-5, the arrows pointing from the independent latent variables to the dependent latent variables are called paths and the numbers on the arrows are called path coefficients. (Later, I will discuss how we get the numbers in Figure 13-5 and their meanings.) Path coefficients are equivalent to the regression coefficients in simple or multiple regression. Recall how we express relationships among variables in regression equations: We put the dependent variable on the left side of the equation and the independent variable(s) on the right side with regression coefficients in front of them. We do the same to express the relationship among latent variables in a LISREL model. The equation for the LISREL model in Figure 13-5 is:

success = 0.65 × busienvi + 0.13 × develop + 0.2 × info_use

In regression analysis, we first select independent and dependent variables, and then we collect data on these variables. Using the data that we collect, we can calculate regression coefficients. This calculation is normally done using computer software. The same basic approach is used for LISREL. Once we decide on the structure of the model (what are the independent and dependent latent variables and what observed variables we will use to measure each latent variable), we then collect data on the observed variables. We input the data along with the structure of the LISREL model into a software package that has a LISREL function. The software will then estimate the path coefficients.

Path coefficients indicate the magnitude of the contribution of each independent latent variable to the dependent latent variable. For the model in Figure 13-5, the path coefficients will allow us to assess the impact of information (one of the independent variables) on business success (the dependent variable) when the contributions of the other independent variables (business environment and business development) are considered along with that of information. I will elaborate on this point later when discussing the results of the study. First, I will give a brief description of the process of the study to illustrate the general process of applying the LISREL methodology.

As stated earlier, the purpose of the study was to measure the contribution of information to business success. Specifically, we examined the impact of information on the success of small manufacturing businesses in Shanghai, China. This relatively narrow focus was necessary to reduce the number of variables involved and to make data collection possible. Assessment of the impact of information cannot be carried out in isolation from the environment in which the information is used. Only when factors other than information are considered along with it is a realistic assessment of the impact of information possible. This is exactly what a LISREL model does. In applying the LISREL approach, initial decisions have to be made about the various factors (independent latent variables) that might contribute to business success (the dependent latent variable). We also have to decide what observed variables can be used to measure the latent variables.

Generally speaking, the model constructed in this initial phase is our hypothesis about the relationships among variables. Once we have entered the data collected and the structure of the model into LISREL software, the software will tell us whether or not the model fits the data. If the initial model does not fit the data, it means that our hypothesis is incorrect. When this happens, we need to revise the model and retest the revised model against the data collected. This process will continue until we find a model that fits the data.[3]

In our study, we constructed an initial model through discussion and consultation with experts in the area. We then collected data on the observed variables from 450 businesses in Shanghai using a questionnaire. The software used for this study was LISREL version 8.12A from Scientific Software International, Inc. After the first analysis, our initial model had to be revised slightly, resulting in the model that appears in Figure 13-5. A detailed, technical discussion of model testing and revision is beyond the scope of this book. Interested readers can refer to our paper (Vaughan and Tague-Sutcliffe, 1997) and books on LISREL such as Jöreskog, K.G. and Sörbom, D. (1993) for detailed discussions of these issues.

The model shown in Figure 13-5 is our final model, which fits the data quite well. The software estimated the path coefficients for the three variables of business environment, business development, and use of information to be 0.65, 0.13, and 0.2 respectively. These coefficients are also displayed in Figure 13-5, which is part of the output from the LISREL software. Like regression coefficients, path coefficients can be either positive or negative. The positive values of these three coefficients mean that the contributions of these factors to business success are positive. The path coefficient of 0.2 for the **info_use** variable (use of information) can be interpreted as follows: If the use of information increases one unit while the values of other variables (i.e., business environment and business development) are held constant, the expected increase in business success is 0.2 unit on average. Similar interpretations can be applied to the business environment and business development factors. Because the path coefficient for business environment (0.65) is the largest among the three, we can say that business environment is the most important factor to business success, followed by the use of information factor. The contribution of business development is the least important among the three factors studied.

LISREL software output also indicates whether the path coefficient is statistically significant or not. This tells us whether the independent variable truly contributes to the dependent variable in the population under study or whether the result is just a coincidence in the particular sample data we collected. The statistical significance of the path coefficient is determined by a t test. As our main interest in this study was to determine the contribution of information use to business success, we need to know if the path coefficient for the **info_use** variable is statistically significant. LISREL output shows the t score for this path coefficient to be 2.75, greater than the critical value of 1.96. This means that the use of information does contribute to business success. Details of the t test for LISREL path coefficients can be found in Hayduk (1987).

The LISREL output contains some other useful messages. Notice that in Figure 13-5 there are numbers on the arrows connecting latent variables to the corresponding observed variables. These numbers show how valid the observed variable is in measuring the latent variable. For example, the number for informal information (0.91) is greater than that for formal information (0.69). This means that the use of informal information is a more valid indicator of information use than the use of formal information. In practical terms, it means that the use of informal information is more important to business success than the use of more formal sources.

In regression analysis, we have a coefficient of determination, R-squared, to measure the percentage of variation in the dependent variable that can be explained by, or attributed to, the variation in the independent variable(s). LISREL also has this R-squared and it has the same meaning. The R-squared for the model in Figure 13-5 is 0.8. This means that 80 percent of the variation in business success can be explained by the variation in business environment, business development, and use of information.

An added benefit of using a mathematical model such as LISREL is the ability to compare different phenomena by comparing the coefficients of the model. We studied both small and medium-sized businesses using LISREL model. A comparison of the coefficients of the two LISREL models revealed similarities and differences between the two types of businesses, which helps us understand the impact of information on business success. See Vaughan (1999) for details of this comparison.

In summary, the LISREL methodology is essentially a way of testing a theory about relationships among variables. It involves the following process:

1. Identify the variables to be used and specify a tentative model that indicates the relationships among variables (typically by a path diagram as shown Figure 13-5).
2. Collect data on the observed variables.
3. Test the model against the data collected using LISREL software.
4. If the model does not fit the data, then revise the model and re-test it until it fits.

Endnotes

1. In Chapter 10, I said that data for ANOVA must be ratio or interval. In fact, this applies only to the dependent variable. The independent variable is always measured in nominal or ordinal scale because it defines the groups being compared.

2. If there are three independent variables, the regression equation is $Y = b_0 + b_1X_1 + b_2X_2 + b_3X_3$. Accordingly, if there are n independent variables, the regression equation is $Y = b_0 + b_1X_1 + b_2X_2 + ... + b_nX_n$.

3. At this point, you may wonder if it ever happens that the model cannot be revised to fit the data. The answer is, not surprisingly, "Yes." A LISREL model is essentially our theory of how variables affect each other and we test our theory using the data we collect. Therefore, if the model cannot be made to fit the data, we just have to accept that our theory is incorrect and we have to start over with a completely new model.

Appendices

Standard Normal Distribution

z score	Probability between mean and z	z score	Probability between mean and z	z score	Probability between mean and z
0	0.0000	1.22	0.3888	1.54	0.4382
0.1	0.0398	1.23	0.3907	1.55	0.4394
0.2	0.0793	1.24	0.3925	1.56	0.4406
0.3	0.1179	1.25	0.3944	1.57	0.4418
0.4	0.1554	1.26	0.3962	1.58	0.4429
0.5	0.1915	1.27	0.3980	1.59	0.4441
0.6	0.2257	1.28	0.3997	1.60	0.4452
0.7	0.2580	1.29	0.4015	1.61	0.4463
0.8	0.2881	1.30	0.4032	1.62	0.4474
0.9	0.3159	1.31	0.4049	1.63	0.4484
1.0	0.3413	1.32	0.4066	1.64	0.4495
1.01	0.3438	1.33	0.4082	1.65	0.4505
1.02	0.3461	1.34	0.4099	1.66	0.4515
1.03	0.3485	1.35	0.4115	1.67	0.4525
1.04	0.3508	1.36	0.4131	1.68	0.4535
1.05	0.3531	1.37	0.4147	1.69	0.4545
1.06	0.3554	1.38	0.4162	1.70	0.4554
1.07	0.3577	1.39	0.4177	1.71	0.4564
1.08	0.3599	1.40	0.4192	1.72	0.4573
1.09	0.3621	1.41	0.4207	1.73	0.4582
1.10	0.3643	1.42	0.4222	1.74	0.4591
1.11	0.3665	1.43	0.4236	1.75	0.4599
1.12	0.3686	1.44	0.4251	1.76	0.4608
1.13	0.3708	1.45	0.4265	1.77	0.4616
1.14	0.3729	1.46	0.4279	1.78	0.4625
1.15	0.3749	1.47	0.4292	1.79	0.4633
1.16	0.3770	1.48	0.4306	1.80	0.4641
1.17	0.3790	1.49	0.4319	1.81	0.4649
1.18	0.3810	1.50	0.4332	1.82	0.4656
1.19	0.3830	1.51	0.4345	1.83	0.4664
1.20	0.3849	1.52	0.4357	1.84	0.4671
1.21	0.3869	1.53	0.4370	1.85	0.4678

z score	Probability between mean and z	z score	Probability between mean and z	z score	Probability between mean and z
1.86	0.4686	1.95	0.4744	2.4	0.4918
1.87	0.4693	1.96	0.4750	2.5	0.4938
1.88	0.4699	1.97	0.4756	2.6	0.4953
1.89	0.4706	1.98	0.4761	2.7	0.4965
1.9	0.4713	1.99	0.4767	2.8	0.4974
1.91	0.4719	2.0	0.4772	2.9	0.4981
1.92	0.4726	2.1	0.4821	3.0	0.4987
1.93	0.4732	2.2	0.4861	4.0	0.5000
1.94	0.4738	2.3	0.4893		

Entries in the table calculated by the author using Microsoft Excel 2000.

Random Number Table

38	94	75	66	84	65	60	54	26	01	26	93	35	41	20
10	05	62	72	55	26	92	80	17	69	80	25	59	23	84
59	70	17	58	86	76	53	95	87	69	20	53	96	76	58
89	81	40	15	44	69	13	09	81	88	45	20	01	98	67
88	96	55	88	22	85	08	11	04	17	40	75	50	90	99
95	46	70	37	85	00	57	71	89	88	93	59	45	57	28
01	30	55	20	28	67	82	87	42	28	09	51	83	31	21
40	74	18	20	70	92	07	19	13	23	17	15	88	40	88
85	35	96	33	70	04	27	02	03	04	43	38	94	13	38
14	77	68	32	37	51	69	18	20	91	14	76	03	52	08
24	07	52	30	33	90	41	57	68	17	08	49	78	39	86
05	20	79	79	09	94	36	66	81	93	02	83	64	73	10
03	06	80	69	97	59	43	16	47	12	71	15	76	10	34
16	35	26	27	28	55	33	19	47	34	36	77	68	69	07
22	48	18	90	53	96	21	67	58	09	65	88	44	83	13
02	51	86	04	40	48	73	54	36	93	02	12	94	19	72
28	37	11	70	99	25	52	29	82	51	87	65	67	64	54
34	98	06	45	89	81	89	54	31	62	03	04	48	70	04
55	04	75	51	80	49	60	17	98	83	30	53	49	83	97
35	23	73	25	90	84	52	18	76	96	16	83	47	41	59
37	00	98	29	57	66	58	84	72	47	46	84	05	59	91
35	92	92	79	70	92	58	94	16	15	55	54	66	33	48
90	10	89	78	40	45	49	25	80	28	95	22	57	69	40
46	25	54	67	11	17	11	43	92	79	30	71	73	93	51
42	77	50	75	89	06	59	54	23	80	21	67	43	43	03
30	67	67	94	38	01	55	96	38	69	23	76	79	15	24
97	80	48	61	09	54	77	72	09	07	71	17	90	18	91
80	72	14	71	77	61	23	94	90	08	89	72	96	76	56
98	08	04	96	78	49	72	56	84	44	07	94	09	94	33
25	13	79	36	66	57	58	93	57	26	83	59	73	26	27

Table generated by the author using Random Number Generation Function from the Data Analysis Toolpak in Microsoft Excel 2000.

Critical Values of Chi-Square

df	0.05	0.01	df	0.05	0.01
1	3.84	6.63	16	26.30	32.00
2	5.99	9.21	17	27.59	33.41
3	7.81	11.34	18	28.87	34.81
4	9.49	13.28	19	30.14	36.19
5	11.07	15.09	20	31.41	37.57
6	12.59	16.81	21	32.67	38.93
7	14.07	18.48	22	33.92	40.29
8	15.51	20.09	23	35.17	41.64
9	16.92	21.67	24	36.42	42.98
10	18.31	23.21	25	37.65	44.31
11	19.68	24.73	26	38.89	45.64
12	21.03	26.22	27	40.11	46.96
13	22.36	27.69	28	41.34	48.28
14	23.68	29.14	29	42.56	49.59
15	25.00	30.58	30	43.77	50.89

Entries in the table calculated by the author using Microsoft Excel 2000.

Critical Values of Pearson r

df	0.05	0.01	df	0.05	0.01
1	0.9969	0.9999	28	0.3610	0.4629
2	0.9500	0.9900	29	0.3550	0.4556
3	0.8783	0.9587	30	0.3494	0.4487
4	0.8114	0.9172	31	0.3440	0.4421
5	0.7545	0.8745	32	0.3388	0.4357
6	0.7067	0.8343	33	0.3338	0.4296
7	0.6664	0.7977	34	0.3291	0.4238
8	0.6319	0.7646	35	0.3246	0.4182
9	0.6021	0.7348	36	0.3202	0.4128
10	0.5760	0.7079	37	0.3160	0.4076
11	0.5529	0.6835	38	0.3120	0.4026
12	0.5324	0.6614	39	0.3081	0.3978
13	0.5140	0.6411	40	0.3044	0.3932
14	0.4973	0.6226	42	0.2973	0.3843
15	0.4821	0.6055	44	0.2907	0.3761
16	0.4683	0.5897	46	0.2845	0.3683
17	0.4555	0.5751	48	0.2787	0.3610
18	0.4438	0.5614	50	0.2732	0.3542
19	0.4329	0.5487	55	0.2609	0.3385
20	0.4227	0.5368	60	0.2500	0.3248
21	0.4132	0.5256	65	0.2404	0.3126
22	0.4044	0.5151	70	0.2319	0.3017
23	0.3961	0.5052	80	0.2172	0.2830
24	0.3882	0.4958	100	0.1946	0.2540
25	0.3809	0.4869	150	0.1593	0.2084
26	0.3739	0.4785	200	0.1381	0.1809
27	0.3673	0.4705	500	0.0875	0.1149

Entries in the table calculated by the author using Microsoft Excel 2000.

Critical Values of t

df	0.05	0.01	df	0.05	0.01
1	12.706	63.656	24	2.064	2.797
2	4.303	9.925	25	2.060	2.787
3	3.182	5.841	26	2.056	2.779
4	2.776	4.604	27	2.052	2.771
5	2.571	4.032	28	2.048	2.763
6	2.447	3.707	29	2.045	2.756
7	2.365	3.499	30	2.042	2.750
8	2.306	3.355	32	2.037	2.738
9	2.262	3.250	34	2.032	2.728
10	2.228	3.169	36	2.028	2.719
11	2.201	3.106	38	2.024	2.712
12	2.179	3.055	40	2.021	2.704
13	2.160	3.012	45	2.014	2.690
14	2.145	2.977	50	2.009	2.678
15	2.131	2.947	60	2.000	2.660
16	2.120	2.921	70	1.994	2.648
17	2.110	2.898	80	1.990	2.639
18	2.101	2.878	100	1.984	2.626
19	2.093	2.861	150	1.976	2.609
20	2.086	2.845	200	1.972	2.601
21	2.080	2.831	500	1.965	2.586
22	2.074	2.819	1000	1.962	2.581
23	2.069	2.807	∞	1.960	2.576

Entries in the table calculated by the author using Microsoft Excel 2000.

Critical Values of F for ANOVA ($\alpha = 0.05$)

Within Group Degrees of Freedom	Between Group Degrees of Freedom					
	1	2	3	4	5	6
1	161.446	199.499	215.707	224.583	230.160	233.988
2	18.513	19.000	19.164	19.247	19.296	19.329
3	10.128	9.552	9.277	9.117	9.013	8.941
4	7.709	6.944	6.591	6.388	6.256	6.163
5	6.608	5.786	5.409	5.192	5.050	4.950
6	5.987	5.143	4.757	4.534	4.387	4.284
7	5.591	4.737	4.347	4.120	3.972	3.866
8	5.318	4.459	4.066	3.838	3.688	3.581
9	5.117	4.256	3.863	3.633	3.482	3.374
10	4.965	4.103	3.708	3.478	3.326	3.217
11	4.844	3.982	3.587	3.357	3.204	3.095
12	4.747	3.885	3.490	3.259	3.106	2.996
13	4.667	3.806	3.411	3.179	3.025	2.915
14	4.600	3.739	3.344	3.112	2.958	2.848
15	4.543	3.682	3.287	3.056	2.901	2.790
16	4.494	3.634	3.239	3.007	2.852	2.741
17	4.451	3.592	3.197	2.965	2.810	2.699
18	4.414	3.555	3.160	2.928	2.773	2.661
19	4.381	3.522	3.127	2.895	2.740	2.628
20	4.351	3.493	3.098	2.866	2.711	2.599
21	4.325	3.467	3.072	2.840	2.685	2.573
22	4.301	3.443	3.049	2.817	2.661	2.549
23	4.279	3.422	3.028	2.796	2.640	2.528
24	4.260	3.403	3.009	2.776	2.621	2.508
25	4.242	3.385	2.991	2.759	2.603	2.490
26	4.225	3.369	2.975	2.743	2.587	2.474
27	4.210	3.354	2.960	2.728	2.572	2.459
28	4.196	3.340	2.947	2.714	2.558	2.445
29	4.183	3.328	2.934	2.701	2.545	2.432
30	4.171	3.316	2.922	2.690	2.534	2.421
40	4.085	3.232	2.839	2.606	2.449	2.336
60	4.001	3.150	2.758	2.525	2.368	2.254
120	3.920	3.072	2.680	2.447	2.290	2.175
∞	3.841	2.996	2.605	2.372	2.214	2.099

Entries in the table calculated by the author using Microsoft Excel 2000.

Critical Values for Tukey's HSD ($\alpha = 0.05$)

Within Group Degrees of Freedom	K = number of groups				
	2	3	4	5	6
5	3.64	4.60	5.22	5.67	6.03
6	3.46	4.34	4.90	5.30	5.63
7	3.34	4.16	4.68	5.06	5.36
8	3.26	4.04	4.53	4.89	5.17
9	3.20	3.95	4.41	4.76	5.02
10	3.15	3.88	4.33	4.65	4.91
11	3.11	3.82	4.26	4.57	4.82
12	3.08	3.77	4.20	4.51	4.75
13	3.06	3.73	4.15	4.45	4.69
14	3.03	3.70	4.11	4.41	4.64
15	3.01	3.67	4.08	4.37	4.59
16	3.00	3.65	4.05	4.33	4.56
17	2.98	3.63	4.02	4.30	4.52
18	2.97	3.61	4.00	4.28	4.49
19	2.96	3.59	3.98	4.25	4.47
20	2.95	3.58	3.96	4.23	4.45
24	2.92	3.53	3.90	4.17	4.37
30	2.89	3.49	3.85	4.10	4.30
40	2.86	3.44	3.79	4.04	4.23
60	2.83	3.40	3.74	3.98	4.16
120	2.80	3.36	3.68	3.92	4.10
∞	2.77	3.31	3.63	3.86	4.03

Abridged from R. P. Runyon & A. Haber (1987). *Fundamentals of Behavioral Statistics*, 6th ed. New York: McGraw-Hill, Table O (p.486). Reprinted with permission of McGraw-Hill.

Bibliography

Agresti, A. and Finlay, B. (1997). *Statistical Methods for the Social Sciences*, 3rd ed. New Jersey, U.S.A.: Prentice Hall.

Conover, W. J. (1980). *Practical Nonparametric Statistics*, 2nd ed., New York: John Wiley & Sons.

Diekhoff, G. M. (1996). *Basic Statistics for the Social and Behavioral Sciences*. New Jersey, U.S.A.: Prentice-Hall.

Dolan, E. and Vaughan, L. (1998). *Electronic Access to Canadian Federal Government Information: How Prepared Are the Depository Libraries?* Ottawa, Canada: Minister of Public Works and Government Services Canada.

Erickson, B. H. and Nosanchuk, T. A. (1992). *Understanding Data*, 2nd ed. Toronto, Canada: University of Toronto Press.

Gonick, L. and Smith, W. (1993). *The Cartoon Guide to Statistics*. New York, U.S.A.: Harper Perennial.

Hayduk, L. (1987). *Structural equation modelling with LISREL: essentials and advances*. Baltimore: The Johns Hopkins University Press.

Hopkins, K. D. and Glass, G. V. (1978). *Basic Statistics for the Behavioral Sciences*. Englewood Cliffs, New Jersey: Prentice-Hall Inc.

Howell, D. C. (1997). *Statistical Methods for Psychology*, 4th ed. Belmont, CA: Duxbury Press.

Jöreskog, K. G. and Sörbom, D. (1993). *LISREL 8: structural equation modeling with the SIMPLIS command language*. Chicago: Scientific Software International, Inc.

Levin, J. and Fox, J. A. (1997). *Elementary Statistics in Social Research*, 7th ed. New York, U.S.A.: Longman.

Qiu, L. (1993). Analytical Searching vs. Browsing in Hypertext Information Retrieval Systems, *The Canadian Journal of Information and Library Science*, 18(4), 1–13.

Rowntree, D. (1981). *Statistics without Tears: A Primer for Non-mathematicians*. London, England: Penguin Books.

Sprinthall, R. C. (1997). *Basic Statistical Analysis*, 5th ed. Boston, U.S.A.: Allyn and Bacon.

SPSS Inc. (1998). *SPSS® Base 8.0 Applications Guide*. Chicago, U.S.A.: SPSS Inc.

Vaughan, L. Q. (1999). The Contribution of Information to Business Success: A LISREL Model Analysis of Manufacturers in Shanghai. *Information Processing & Management*, 35(2), 193–208.

Vaughan, L. Q. (1997). Information Search Patterns of Business Communities: A Comparison between Small and Medium-sized Businesses, *Reference and User Services Quarterly*, 37(1), 71–78.

Vaughan, L. Q. and Tague-Sutcliffe, J. (1997). Measuring the Impact of Information on Development: A LISREL-Based Study of Small Business in Shanghai, *Journal of the American Society for Information Science*, 48(10), 917–931.

Vaughan, L. Q., Tague-Sutcliffe, J., and Tripp, P. (1996). The Value of the Public Library to Small Businesses, *RQ*, 36(2), 262–269.

Walsh, A. (1990). *Statistics for the Social Sciences: With Computer Applications*. New York, U.S.A.: Harper & Row.

About the Author

Dr. Liwen Qiu Vaughan earned her Ph.D. in Library and Information Science from the University of Western Ontario in 1991. Her strong interest in statistical analysis, combined with her ability to explain difficult concepts in clear and understandable ways, has led to a successful career as an educator. She has taught courses in statistics for over ten years in various degree programs including library and information science, journalism, and business administration and to students at all levels (undergraduate, Master, and Ph.D.). Dr. Vaughan has extensive experience using statistical analysis in information science research. Her research, published in numerous information science journals, has employed a variety of statistical methods. Her paper on using the Markov model to analyze hypertext information systems, published in JASIS, has attracted inquiries from Ph.D. students around the world. Recently, she successfully used the LISREL model (an advanced statistical method new to information science research) to quantitatively measure the impact of information on business development.

Index

A

Alternate hypotheses, 60, 77
ANOVA (analysis of variance),
    125–138
    factorial, 164, 169–171
    homogeneity requirements, 139
    logic, 126–129
    one-way, 170
    power, 161
    procedure, 129–131
    selection of, 160, 161
    two-way, 163–170
    using software, 131–133
Association, hypotheses of, 157,
    160–161
Average. *see* Mean
Average deviation from the mean,
    36

B

Bargraphs
    histograms, 20–24
    horizontal, *17*
    vertical, *16, 18*
Bell curves, 24
Biases
    in sampling, 71–73
    response rates, 7
    sampling, 89
    self-selection, 71–72
Bimodal distributions, *30,* 30–31
Bivariate regressions, 171

C

*Canadian Journal of Information
    and Library Science,* 164
Categories, labeling, 2
Causation, and correlation, 100–102,
    143
Central tendencies
    measure selection algorithm, *32*
    measures of, 25–33
    skew distributions, 40–41
Chance
    and confidence intervals, 56
    and probability, 47–48
Chi-square test (χ^2), 75–91
    critical values table, 81–83, 189
    logic of, 75–78
    requirements for, 88–91
    sampling, 89
    selection of, 161
    sensitivity of scores, 80–81, 89
    SPSS, 84–88
Coding, SPSS, 90–91
Coefficient of determination (R^2),
    108, 172, 181
Coin tosses, 47–48
Comparisons, interval data, 3–4
Confidence intervals, 54–58, 58–62
Confidence levels, 56, 58
Contingency tables, 77, 78, 86
Conversions
    data types, 5–7
    file transfers, 11
    guidelines, 161
    missing data, 14

More Great Books
From Information Today, Inc.

ARIST 34
Annual Review of Information Science and Technology

Edited by Professor Martha E. Williams

ANNUAL REVIEW OF
INFORMATION
SCIENCE AND
TECHNOLOGY

asis

MARTHA E. WILLIAMS, EDITOR
VOLUME 34 1999

Since 1966, the *Annual Review of Information Science and Technology (ARIST)* has been continuously at the cutting edge in contributing a useful and comprehensive view of the broad field of information science and technology. ARIST reviews numerous topics within the field and ultimately provides this annual source of ideas, trends, and references to the literature. Published by Information Today, Inc. on behalf of the American Society for Information Science (ASIS), ARIST Volume 34 (1999) is the latest volume in this legendary series. The newest edition of ARIST covers the following topics:

• The History of Documentation and Information Science (Colin Burke) • Applications of Machine Learning in Information Retrieval (Sally Jo Cunningham, Jamie Littin, and Ian Witten) • Privacy and Digital Information (Philip Doty) • Cognitive Information Retrieval (Peter Ingwersen) • Text Mining (Walter Trybula) • Methodologies for Human Behavioral Research (Peiling Wang) • Measuring the Internet (Robert Williams and Bob Molyneux) • Infometric Laws (Concepcion Wilson and William Hood) • Using and Reading Scholarly Literature (Donald W. King and Carol Tenopir) • Literature Dynamics: Studies on Growth, Diffusion, and Epidemics (Albert Tabah).

Hardbound • ISBN 1-57387-093-5

ASIST Members $79.95   **Non-Members $99.95**

Introductory Concepts in Information Science

Melanie J. Norton

Melanie J. Norton presents a unique introduction to the practical and theoretical concepts of information science while examining the impact of the Information Age on society. Drawing on recent research into the field, as well as from scholarly and trade publications, the monograph provides a brief history of information science and coverage of key topics, including communications and cognition, information retrieval, bibliometrics, modeling, economics, information policies, and the impact of information technology on modern management. This is an essential volume for graduate students, practitioners, and any professional who needs a solid grounding in the field of information science.

Hardbound • ISBN 1-57387-087-0

ASIST Members $31.60   **Non-Members $39.50**

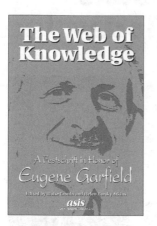

The Web of Knowledge
A Festschrift in Honor
of Eugene Garfield

Edited by Blaise Cronin
and Helen Barsky Atkins

Dr. Eugene Garfield, the founder of the Institute for Scientific Information (ISI), has devoted his life to the creation and development of the multidisciplinary Science Citation Index. The index, a unique resource for scientists, scholars, and researchers in virtually every field of intellectual endeavor, has been the foundation for a multidisciplinary research community. This new ASIST monograph is the first to comprehensively address the history, theory, and practical applications of the Science Citation Index and to examine its impact on scholarly and scientific research 40 years after its inception. In bringing together the analyses, insights, and reflections of more than 35 leading lights, editors Cronin and Atkins have produced both a comprehensive survey of citation indexing and analysis and a beautifully realized tribute to Eugene Garfield and his vision.

Hardbound • ISBN 1-57387-099-4

ASIST Members $39.60   **Non-Members $49.50**

Intelligent Technologies
in Library and Information
Service Applications

F.W. Lancaster and Amy Warner

Librarians and library school faculty have been experimenting with artificial intelligence (AI) and expert systems for 30 years, but there has been no comprehensive survey of the results available until now. In this carefully researched monograph, authors Lancaster and Warner report on the applications of AI technologies in library and information services, assessing their effectiveness, reviewing the relevant literature, and offering a clear-eyed forecast of future use and impact. Includes almost 500 bibliographic references.

Hardbound • ISBN 1-57387-103-6

ASIST Members $31.60   **Non-Members $39.50**

Knowledge Management
for the Information Professional

Edited by T. Kanti Srikantaiah
and Michael Koenig

Written from the perspective of the information community, this book examines the business community's recent enthusiasm for Knowledge Management (KM). With contributions from 26 leading KM practitioners, academicians, and information professionals, editors Srikantaiah and Koenig bridge the gap between two distinct perspectives, equipping information professionals with the tools to make a broader and more effective contribution in developing KM systems and creating a Knowledge Management culture within their organizations.

Hardbound • ISBN 1-57387-079-X

ASIST Members $35.60   **Non-Members $44.50**

Knowledge Management
The Bibliography

Compiled by Paul Burden

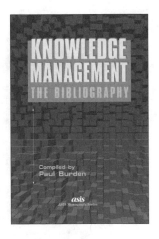

Knowledge Management (KM) is a holistic process by which an organization may effectively gather, evaluate, share, analyze, integrate, and use information from both internal and external sources. *Knowledge Management: The Bibliography* is the first comprehensive reference to the literature available for the individual interested in KM, and features citations to over 1500 published articles, 150+ Web sites, and more than 400 books. Organized by topic area (i.e., "KM and Intranets," "KM and Training," "KM and eCommerce"), this work is a natural companion volume to the ASIS monograph, *Knowledge Management for the Information Professional*, and an important new tool for anyone charged with contributing to or managing an organization's intellectual assets.

Softbound • ISBN: 1-57387-101-X

ASIS Members $18.00   **Non-Members $22.50**

Editorial PEER REVIEW
Its Strengths and Weaknesses
Ann C. Weller

This important book is the first to provide an in-depth analysis of the peer review process in scholarly publishing. Author Weller (Associate Professor and Deputy Director at the Library of the Health Sciences, University of Illinois at Chicago) offers a carefully researched, systematic review of published studies of editorial peer review in the following broad categories: general studies of rejection rates, studies of editors, studies of authors, and studies of reviewers. The book concludes with an examination of new models of editorial peer review intended to enhance the scientific communication process as it moves from a print to an electronic environment. *Editorial Peer Review* is an essential monograph for editors, reviewers, publishers, professionals from learned societies, writers, scholars, and librarians who purchase and disseminate scholarly material.

Hardbound • ISBN 1-57387-100-1

ASIST Members $35.60   **Non-Members $44.50**

Information Management
for the Intelligent Organization,
Second Edition
Chun Wei Choo

The intelligent organization is one that is skilled at marshalling its information resources and capabilities, transforming information into knowledge, and using this knowledge to sustain and enhance its performance in a restless environment. The objective of this newly updated and expanded book is to develop an understanding of how an organization may manage its information processes more effectively in order to achieve these goals. This book is a must read for senior managers and administrators, information managers, information specialists and practitioners, information technologists, and anyone whose work in an organization involves acquiring, creating, organizing, or using knowledge.

hardbound • ISBN 1-57387-057-9

ASIST Members $31.60   **Non-Members $39.50**

The Evolving Virtual Library II
Practical and Philosophical Perspectives
Edited by Laverna M. Saunders

This new edition of *The Evolving Virtual Library* documents how libraries of all types are changing with the integration of the Internet and the Web, electronic resources, and computer networks. It provides a summary of trends over the last 5 years, new developments in networking, case studies of creating digital content delivery systems for remote users, applications in K-12 and public libraries, and a vision of things to come. The contributing experts are highly regarded in their specialties. The information is timely and presents a snapshot of what libraries are dealing with in the new millennium.

Hardbound • ISBN 1-57387-070-6 • $39.50

Teaching with Technology
Rethinking Tradition
Edited by Les Lloyd

This latest informative volume from Les Lloyd includes contributions from leading experts on the use of technology in higher education. Four sections are included: Cross-Discipline Use of Technology, The Web as a Tool in Specific Disciplines, Technology Management for Faculty and Administration, and Techniques for Enhancing Teaching in Cross-Discipline Courses. If your college or university needs to be on the cutting edge of the technology revolution, this book is highly recommended.

Hardbound • ISBN 1-57387-068-4 • $39.50

Internet Blue Pages
The Guide to Federal Government Web Sites, 2001—2002 Edition

By Laurie Andriot

*"A handy, useful guide to federal government information
...comprehensive...authoritative...recommended."*

—*CHOICE*

Internet Blue Pages (IBP) is the leading guide to federal government information on the Web. *IBP 2001-2002* includes over 1,800 annotated agency listings, arranged in U.S. Government Manual style to help you find the information you need. Entries include agency name and URL, function or purpose of selected agencies, and links from agency home pages. With double the coverage of the previous edition, *IBP* now includes federal courts, military libraries, Department of Energy libraries, Federal Reserve banks, presidential libraries, national parks, and Social Security offices. A companion Web site features regularly updated agency links.

Softbound • ISBN 0-910965-43-9 • $34.95

Great Scouts!
CyberGuides for Subject Searching on the Web

By Nora Paul and Margot Williams
Edited by Paula Hane
Foreword by Barbara Quint

Great Scouts! is a cure for information overload. Authors Nora Paul (The Poynter Institute) and Margot Williams (*The Washington Post*) direct readers to the very best subject-specific, Web-based information resources. Thirty chapters cover specialized "CyberGuides" selected as the premier Internet sources of information on business, education, arts and entertainment, science and technology, health and medicine, politics and government, law, sports, and much more. With its expert advice and evaluations of information and link content, value, currency, stability, and usability, *Great Scouts!* takes you "beyond search engines"—and directly to the top sources of information for your topic. As a reader bonus, the authors are maintaining a Web page featuring links to all the sites covered in the book.

Softbound • ISBN 0-910965-27-7 • $24.95

The Modem Reference, 4th Edition
The Complete Guide to PC Communications
By Michael A. Banks

"If you can't find the answer to a telecommunications problem here, there probably isn't an answer."

—Lawrence Blasko, *The Associated Press*

Now in its 4th edition, this popular handbook explains the concepts behind computer data, data encoding, and transmission; providing practical advice for PC users who want to get the most from their online operations. In his uniquely readable style, author and techno-guru Mike Banks *(The Internet Unplugged)* takes readers on a tour of PC data communications technology, explaining how modems, fax machines, computer networks, and the Internet work. He provides an in-depth look at how data is communicated between computers all around the world, demystifying the terminology, hardware, and software. *The Modem Reference* is a must-read for students, professional online users, and all computer users who want to maximize their PC fax and data communications capability.

Softbound • ISBN 0-910965-36-6 • $29.95

Electronic Styles
A Handbook for Citing Electronic Information
By Xia Li and Nancy Crane

The second edition of the best-selling guide to referencing electronic information and citing the complete range of electronic formats includes text-based information, electronic journals and discussion lists, Web sites, CD-ROM and multimedia products, and commercial online documents.

Softbound • ISBN 1-57387-027-7 • $19.99

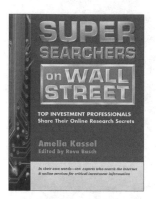

Super Searchers on Wall Street
Top Investment Professionals
Share Their Online Research Secrets

By Amelia Kassel
Edited by Reva Basch

Through her probing interviews, Amelia Kassel reveals the online secrets of 10 leading financial industry research experts. You'll learn how information professionals find and analyze market and industry data, as well as how online information is used by brokerages, stock exchanges, investment banks, and individual investors to make critical investment decisions. The Wall Street Super Searchers direct you to important sites and sources, illuminate the trends that are revolutionizing financial research, and help you use online research as part of a powerful investment strategy. As a reader bonus, a directory of top sites and sources is hyperlinked and periodically updated on the Web.

Softbound • ISBN 0-910965-42-0 • $24.95

Super Searchers on Health & Medicine
The Online Secrets of
Top Health & Medical Researchers

By Susan M. Detwiler
Edited by Reva Basch

With human lives depending on them, skilled medical researchers rank among the best online searchers in the world. In *Super Searchers on Health & Medicine*, medical librarians, clinical researchers, health information specialists, and physicians explain how they combine traditional sources with the best of the Net to deliver just what the doctor ordered. If you use the Internet and online databases to answer important health and medical questions, these Super Searchers will help guide you around the perils and pitfalls to the best sites, sources, and techniques. As a reader bonus, "The Super Searchers Web Page" provides links to the most important Internet resources for health and medical researchers.

Softbound • ISBN 0-910965-44-7 • $24.95

For a complete catalog, contact:

Information Today, Inc.

143 Old Marlton Pike, Medford, NJ 08055 • 609/654-6266
email: custserv@infotoday.com • Web site: www.infotoday.com